The Best of
SLO NightWriters
in Tolosa Press
2009-2013

Edited by

Judythe A. Guarnera

SLO NightWriters
P.O. Box 6241
Los Osos, CA 93412
www.slonightwriters.org

Printed in the United States of America

ISBN-13: 978-1499717549

ISBN-10: 1499717547

EDITORIAL STAFF

EXECUTIVE EDITOR
Judythe A. Guarnera

ASSOCIATE MANUSCRIPT EDITORS
Christine Ahern

Paul Alan Fahey

Jean Moelter

Susan Vasquez

TECHNICAL EDITOR
Steve Kliewer

PUBLISHING CONSULTANT
Tom Snow

COVER PHOTO
Dennis Eamon Young Photo

PUBLISHER
SLO NightWriters

DEDICATION

This anthology is lovingly dedicated to Anne Peterson, who played a key role in the early days of SLO NightWriters. In the ensuing years she assumed a variety of tasks, from president to newsletter editor. When it became difficult for Anne to attend meetings, she continued to contribute with her "Ana Nimiti" column in the NW newsletter. Then she joined the editorial committee for the newly founded NightWriter column in the Tolosa Press publications and served in that capacity for five years.

Thanks to Anne's editing assistance, more than 140 NightWriter columns were published in the Tolosa Press Newspapers: *SLO City News, Coast News,* and *Bay News.*

You made it happen, Anne, and for that we are grateful.

INTRODUCTION

Throughout my adult life, the idea of writing a column for a newspaper or magazine fascinated me. Several times I drafted a proposal for a local publication, but never followed through, because the idea of having to be creative on deadline seemed overwhelming.

After I joined SLO NightWriters and found myself surrounded with like-minded individuals who loved to write and to be published, the idea of a column resurfaced. I approached Susan Tuttle, the NW President at the time, with a proposal for a bi-monthly column in the local Tolosa Press publications. We met with Christopher Gardner, Executive Editor at Tolosa Press. We assured him that the work of NW members would be edited and ready to go when it reached his desk. In addition, each piece would include a photo of the author taken by member Dennis Eamon Young, photographer and current president of SLO NightWriters.

The first call for submissions went out in January of 2009. The editorial committee, which included Willy Bruijns, Paul Fahey, Anne Peterson, and yours truly, read and edited the pieces that came in. Six of these were sent to Tolosa. I received an immediate e-mail saying, "I like them all. Let's go." That was the beginning of a relationship that worked for NW, Tolosa Press, and our members.

The twice-a-month column fulfilled one of the goals of SLO NightWriters, which is to advance the writing of its members and to help them add to their publication credits. For those who had never been published, the column was an opportunity to practice submitting—carefully editing and following specific, professional submission guidelines. Since the committee was dedicated to supporting the membership, they often offered guidance that helped the authors improve their work to make it publishable.

I know I speak for the editorial committee when I say that the willingness of the authors to accept constructive criticism and to learn from it made the column work. Over 140 pieces—flash fiction, non-fiction, essays, interviews, and memoir—were published during the first five years of the column. I am proud to say that Tolosa always had edited stories in the pipeline.

We couldn't stop there. The discussion of a NW anthology had been on the table for a while. Why not select the best of the columns that had been published in Tolosa for our very own anthology? And that's exactly what we did.

After a great deal of consideration, the selections were made. SLO NightWriters is honored to publish its first anthology. Hopefully this volume will be one of many highlighting the work of its membership.

It has been a pleasure to work with the reliable and erudite editorial committee, the NW Board, and all the industrious members who took the challenge and submitted their work. I confess I love to be published, but sharing the joy of others being published knocked my socks off.

I would be remiss if I did not express my deep gratitude to the Anthology Committee: Christine Ahern, Paul Fahey, Jean Moelter, Tom Snow; Susan Vasquez; and my husband, Steve Kliewer, who jumped right in with the technical advice I so sorely needed. Without the support of each of you, this anthology could not have come to fruition.

Remember: To be published, one must submit, and to submit one must write. My wish is for on-going productive writing for the authors showcased herein, and happy reading to those of you who pick up *The Best of SLO NightWriters in Tolosa Press 2009-2013.*

~Judythe A. Guarnera, Editor

FORWARD

"There is nothing to writing. All you do is sit down at a typewriter and bleed."
                                                      ~ Ernest Hemingway

It was a rather innocuous first meeting when Judy Guarnera and Susan Tuttle came strolling into the Tolosa Press office with an idea for a column. The newspaper business makes one skeptical and I have had my share of aspiring writers wanting a column only to disappear after one or two feeble attempts, so I was reluctant to jump in.

It quickly became evident this was different. They were representing a local writing organization called SLO NightWriters. I vaguely knew of them through their association with the annual Central Coast Writers' Conference, but I would soon become a big fan of this organization.

Their idea was simple. Help writers write, edit, polish, and publish their work. Tolosa Press was fortunate enough that they chose us to fulfill the final task. We held them to a regular word count and saved the space knowing and trusting that each and every column would be wonderful. And since 2009 it was my great pleasure to introduce San Luis Obispo to splendid writing and wonderful writers.

Looking over the list of authors and their works contained herein, I am humbled to have played a slight role in this anthology and honored to help the printed word survive.

Christopher Gardner
Founding Editor
Tolosa Press

ACKNOWLEDGMENTS

Heart-felt thanks to Tolosa Press for its support of SLO NightWriters, our local writing organization. From 2009 until 2013, over 140 columns featuring the work of SLO NightWriters were published in the Tolosa publications—*SLO City News, Coast News,* and *Bay News.*

Kudos go to the SLO NightWriters Board, which wholeheartedly supported this endeavor from the beginning, with a special thank you to President Dennis Eamon Young, who made this anthology a reality.

An extra thank you to the editorial committee, which made sure there was always a supply of stories for the column.

The committee would also like to thank the many gifted writers who submitted their work for publication. You were the heart and soul of the column and it is your work that fills the pages of this anthology.

~Anthology Committee, *The Best of SLO NightWriters in Tolosa Press 2009-2013*

CONTENTS

A Holiday Collection

CONTEST WINNERS

For twenty-five years SLO NightWriters has sponsored an annual writing contest. From its beginnings as a members-only, local contest, it now boasts international contestants and is known as the Golden Quill Awards.

Paul Alan Fahey

CARLOTTA'S NECKLACE
(A Nod to Hitchcock)

Dearest Marnie,

Only now that I've buried my husband in the family plot, do I dare speak about the trouble with Harry and the notorious Carlotta Valdes. I confess, dear cousin, our marriage was not a happy one. We were two souls adrift on a stormy sea with no lifeboat in sight, actors memorizing lines yet crippled by stage fright, unable to speak. Then one morning, my suspicion about Harry and Carlotta surfaced. I was in the day room writing letters when I discovered a topaz medallion on a gold chain hidden in a desk drawer.

Carlotta had worn that necklace to tea at Manderley. You met her last spring at our costume ball, remember? So rich and strange yet determined to seduce Harry and sabotage our union. Poor Carlotta. She never realized she'd got hold of the wrong man.

That evening, I confronted Harry about the necklace. Contrite and tearful, he begged for a second chance. And for a while, our lives regained some sense of normalcy. We lunched on the terrace, rode horses on the downs and played scrabble in the evenings. But unfortunately, the lure of romantic love proved too great for Harry. Put simply, the man was spellbound.

One night I accidentally picked up the bedroom extension and overheard Carlotta ask my husband, "Guess who'll be under Capricorn tomorrow, love?" My mind raced.

January third was Harry's birthday. I suddenly realized who Capricorn was. I wanted Carlotta dead and out of our lives. Forever.

The following Tuesday, in a frenzy, I followed the pair to Jamaica Inn, thirty miles north by northwest of London. Mr. and Mrs. Smith had booked number seventeen, a small suite of rooms on the second floor. It was then I made up my mind. Harry would have to go. Marnie, just think of your fear of bright red and those wicked thunderstorms, and I'm sure you'll understand what drove me to such a state. Late that afternoon I cruised through Manderley's iron gates, ready to activate my plan.

After dinner Harry seemed unusually pensive, and I had the strangest feeling he knew I'd trailed them to the inn. Yet how could he? I'd been ever so careful not to draw attention, to slip quietly past the innkeeper, skim the register and leave unseen. My imagination, perhaps, but a shadow of a doubt lingered.

We retired at eleven, and in the early hours I heard Harry wake beside me and pad across the carpet to the hall. I rose quietly and followed a few feet behind him to the second landing. A little nudge on my part and . . . well, I must say, watching my husband's crumpled body turn somersaults down the thirty-nine steps did wonders for my vertigo. Remember my childhood, Marnie, always fearful, unable to tread the cliff path or gaze upon the rocks below? Not anymore, dear. Wishing you well, I remain,

Your loving cousin,

Rebecca

Manderley

Cornwall, England

January 12, 1940

Willy Bruijns

GIRL TALK

The only rule was you couldn't tell anyone. That's what you'd said, that first night when I took you home and we made the double-wide buck on its blocks. Don't tell anyone, understand? Not anyone, you'd said. Because of your custody battle, you'd said. Because of your kids.

Heck, why would I tell? I was just looking for a good time, having spent the last eighteen months with other women in orange suits. And we did have a good time, didn't we? I knew right away we would, I could tell from the way you looked at me that night in the bar, from the way your gaze traveled slowly down my body and up again, a half-smile pulling at the corner of your mouth.

The next morning you said it again. Don't tell anyone, you'd said. It's all I ask of you. I need my kids here. I just nodded, my lips busy tracing the outline of your ear. That morning we took our time and made the trailer sway, and I knew you'd be back.

And I felt good, that day. The whole day I felt great.

So I called Tracy that night. Guess what, I said. What, she said. And I told her.

How was I to know that she'd tell Erica? Tracy is my best friend, I asked her not to tell anyone. But, when you get your hair done like Tracy did the next morning, you talk, you know? Especially when Erica does your color. It takes a long time, and Erica has this way of asking. Before you know, you tell her all your secrets. Or those of your friends. Know what I mean?

I don't know how it got from Erica to your ex, but I am sorry that she burst into the trailer like that, camera in hand. She sniffed the air like a coon dog. I shouldn't have smoked that joint, I know it made you nervous, me being a parolee and all. But, hey, a camera can't catch the air, just the picture. I tried to cheer you up, say that it wouldn't do any harm, but I thought it looked bad with all those bottles on the floor, clothes everywhere.

Today you had the hearing.

And here you are outside my door, shaking the trailer again, only now I don't like it. I guess the hearing didn't go so well. I'm not opening the door, not even when you ask me so sweetly, in a voice I can't trust, all sing-song and bedroom soft, reminding me what the only rule was. Asking me, how hard could it have been to keep my trap shut? Huh, baby? How hard was that, one teensy li'l rule? Huh?

It won't be long before your voice will rise and your gently tapping finger will be a banging fist. I just hope the door will hold.

Paul Alan Fahey

SLENDER THREAD

The lights from the pier pulled him closer to shore. His legs grew numb, his arms heavy. His ears rang from the wind and the slap of freezing waves. He knew he had to stay focused, keep moving. He heard a buoy clang in unison with the mournful sound of an offshore foghorn. He pushed on, stroke by stroke.

It wouldn't be long before the guards discovered his absence, sounded the alarms. He'd seen it all before from his cell. Coastguard cutters streaming into the bay, their searchlights scanning the water, covering every inch of spray from the Rock to the mainland. Thankfully, the fog was on his side tonight.

He glanced over his shoulder to the middle of the bay, to the place called Alcatraz, its yellow eyes blinking through the thick mist, and then he turned back to the pier, his thoughts on Roe. Her skin so pale, even the slightest pressure left its mark. "The fair Rowena," he'd call her, and then he'd touch her face and smile as the redness began a journey up her neck just below her jaw, the spot he loved most.

His fingers grew numb. He feared the advent of cramps, the death knell of hypothermia, but he kept on, his hands chopping through the foam, the pier moving toward him, its orange lights bobbing through the haze.

Out of breath, he aimed for a piling and slipped, unable to get a grip. He tried again, willed his arms up and around the post. He stayed there hugging his lifeline.

A clock somewhere chimed eleven, the last hour of 1947 and two hours since he'd made his escape. With renewed strength, he pulled himself up the ladder and onto the pier. He lay there under the stars. Exhausted.

Suddenly, there it was above him. Their constellation. His and Roe's. Not an official formation but their own made-up cluster. "We'll draw comfort from the stars," Roe had said. "At night, we'll always be together."

Imagining a ball of thread unwinding from the heavens, he forced himself up and took hold of the celestial string. He walked on.Coit Tower came into view, and he knew where he was, grateful for a beacon that focused his quest.

He thought of Roe's last letter. "I've tried," she wrote, "but I've met someone else, a man like you who is kind and gentle." It was then he understood what had to be done.

At her porch, he let go of the thread. It had done its work. He was home.

He rang the bell.

"Coming," Roe called, her voice competing with a grandfather clock striking twelve.

Who could she be expecting at this late hour, Mr. Kind and Gentle? He laughed.

Roe opened the door. Her lips moved, yet she made no sound. The blood rushed up her neck as she stepped backward.

He followed her inside. His fingers reached for the spot he loved most, then they closed around it. "Happy New Year, darling."

Christine Ahern

THE BURGUNDY ROOM

A perfect storm is what happens when opposing forces of nature meet with disastrous results. I have weathered my share of these storms. As when I have been forced to perform with an incompatible leading man, or an impossible director or an improbable script. But I don't expect it to happen at Tito's. Between myself and an infant maître d.

"I have a reservation." I stamp my foot just hard enough to cause an elegant click on the tile floor. "Doesn't that mean anything anymore?"

"I can check again, Ma'am but I'm pretty sure I don't have a table reserved for you," the maître d says while a line of young starlets flows past us like a river of precious jewels.

"I am Scarlet Hamilton. *The* Scarlet Hamilton."

He flips too quickly through several pages of his book while he glances from side to side. Is he looking for my table or someone to help get this crazy old woman off his back?

"I am meeting my manager here at three."

"Your manager?"

"Sylvester Morgenstern. *The* Sylvester Morgenstern."

"Ah." He flips again. And glances again.

"What are you looking for?" I ask and slam my palm on the book. His silly, blue eyes go wide. "Are you looking for my table or an excuse for losing my reservation?"

"Um…"

"Oh, for heaven's sake." I step into the dining room and glance around.

I miss the elegant glow this room used to have when it was decorated with circular burgundy booths and deep purple theater carpet. The room gleams much too brightly now with white table cloths and steel everything else.

"Sylvester," I delicately yell. Heads turn. I smile at their curious faces. Yes, I *am* Scarlet Hamilton. And, yes, I *am* a client of Sylvester Morgenstern's. "Sylvester Morgenstern," I repeat.

I feel a touch at my elbow. "May I assist you?"

I look the man up and down. Blue-gray hair, nice suit. Finally. An adult. "Yes, actually. I have a reservation and the child at the front desk has lost it. Or doesn't know what one is. I'm not sure." I flick my cashmere shawl across my chest and feel it fall gracefully against my back. I touch my earlobe and diamond earring. "My name…"

"Oh, Ms. Hamilton. You don't need to tell me your name." He smiles at me and bows as he takes my elbow. "We have your table ready. Please excuse Jeremy. He's new here. Still learning all the fine nuances of being a maître d."

"Well," I say with a gracious smile, "I wish him luck."

I am led past tables surrounded by perfectly attired people and plates sprinkled with perfectly arranged morsels of what I assume to be food. I stop and point at a pink hockey puck on a circle of green leaves. "What is that you have there?"

The woman seems truly surprised by my question. "Salmon mousse. On arugula."

"Ah. Well, I don't think I will be having that."

The nice man pulls aside a heavy curtain and bows again. "This way, Ms. Hamilton. Your table is ready. I will direct Mr. Morgenstern here when he arrives."

I slide into the burgundy booth. He flips on the solitary lamp in the middle of the table. It casts a lovely glow that falls across my hands and blends away some of the bend of my fingers. I touch my hair at my temple. "Thank you, sir," I say. "You are a gentleman. May I have a martini while I wait?"

He bows again and glides out of the room. The curtain falls into place and I am alone. Mine is the only booth in the room, the only table. There seem to be boxes of some kind stacked against one wall. That is certainly odd. Perhaps they are preparing for a large party. I attended many a large party here in the day. In *my* day.

"Mother?"

Fingers wrap around my wrist. I lift my head from the table. I touch my wet cheek. "Oh heavens, I must have fallen asleep." I laugh. It takes a moment for my eyes to adjust to the soft light in the burgundy room. "Hello, dear," I say. "Have you come to join me for lunch?"

"Yes." She smiles at me and combs her fingers through my hair. "I've ordered us each a steak and baked potato. How does that sound?"

"Perfect," I say. "Just perfect."

Kirsty Jenkins

HUMANITY

The desire for food had long since left her but the thirst was terrible. There had been some water at first but she had drunk it all. Hadn't even thought about it, he had always come back before. Even when the whiskey fumes were heavy on his breath, when his fumbling hands and clumsy feet met the wall as often as their target, when he had broken her ribs and closed one eye, when he had stumbled out yelling, "Stay here you stupid bitch," he had always come back.

This time he wasn't coming back, part of her knew, though the other part still hoped. The part that was shackled to him despite everything, a primal bond that wasn't easily broken. Something deeper in her than the polish learned in this alien world knew that you didn't just give up on each other.

Now this social soul was stranded.

It was dark, the weight of blackness broken only by a narrow crack between the door and its frame. She stared at that nearly all of the time, partly to know if it was day or night, but also to have a fixed point that prevented her from losing herself in a black hole. At night, when the crack disappeared, loneliness seeped in. She felt like a petal torn from a flower: without form or function.

Sometimes there were sounds outside: cars in the distance; voices; once, footsteps coming cruelly close before fading away again. That time she had tried to make a noise but her parched throat could not oblige.

Lying still for hours and days caused an ache in her body that exercise never had. Memories tormented her, of running, taking delight in moving her body, or of lying on soft blankets instead of damp concrete.

She heard a noise. She lifted her head. Tilting it, she tried desperately to hear something again, to prove that it was real. She did hear it. It was footsteps, more than one person, getting closer.

This time she would not stay silent, even if her voice must. Straining and heaving, she stood up. Forcing seized-up muscles into action she moved to the door. Feeling a straggle of fresh air through the gap energized her. She threw her body against the door again and again, pounding and scrambling, clawing at the obstinate handle.

The voice that spoke suddenly was close. Her efforts had worked. She stayed very still.

"It was coming from in here. There's somebody behind the door."

The noises of struggle switched sides but when the door finally flew open it was still unexpected. The light assaulted her eyes causing a pain so intense that she almost fell over, and at first could not see her savior. She could hear him, though.

"Look, it's a dog. Poor thing looks half dead. We need to get her to a vet."

Hands, more gentle than she knew was possible, lifted and carried her.

Susan Tuttle

SYMMETRY

Sweat rivered down Ana'hia's spider-wrinkled face. She gasped for breath in the smothering heat as the Arcanum women lit the sacred candles, insignificant flames against the brilliance spilling through the cavern's entrance. A hundred years, she thought, and still night won't fall.

Surili placed the seven-branched Withe wand on the altar. It was an empty ritual without the words. Still, Ana'hia stepped to the stone slab, ready to perform it yet again. Perhaps this time...

"Ana'hia!"

A deep male voice echoed from the stone walls. A tall youth supported an ancient desiccate of a man across the cavern. Ana'hia gasped.

"How dare you come here, Dag'ad? Have not arrogant Archimage men caused enough harm? Begone!"

"The Archimage has fallen; Elel and I are the last. We return this."

Dag'ad held out the Arcanum's Sacred Book of Ritual, stolen a hundred years before. Ana'hia took it in reverent hands.

"At last," she breathed, "Arcanum women can bring back the Night."

"We must perform the ritual together."

"Never!"

"But only in unity can we restore Balance."

"No man will again defile the Night Ritual." Ana'hia's voice shuddered with prophecy. "The Arcanum alone will restore Balance!"

"Ana'hia." Dag'ad stumbled forward. "You are wrong."

"Silence!"

Elel took a step forward. Surili ran down the steps, shoved Dag'ad to his knees and struck Elel a blow that laid him unconscious.

Ana'hia held the copper Hecatomb aloft and read aloud the Power Spell. A strengthening glow emanated from the bowl. She set it down and took up the Withe.

"Listen!" Dag'ad's ancient fingers talon-crooked. He fell on his side. "It takes both—" He clutched his chest. "My heart," he whispered, and died.

Ana'hia looked at him and smiled. She fluttered the Withe; a Sun effigy hovered over the Hecatomb then slowly sank out of sight.

"It is done," she intoned.

The Arcanum women watched in reverent silence as the intense light of Eternal Day faded. And Night fell.

****

An icy wave shuddered through Ana'hia, a cold she had never known. It had deepened in the six months since Eternal Day ended and Night began. Ponds had grown hard; rime frosted fields; new crops stopped growing. She understood at last the inextricable nexus that created symmetry and maintained life.

"But Elel, we need each other." Ana'hia leaned closer to the fire, seeking warmth.

"I am sorry," Elel murmured. "I wish I could, but—"

"You are man age." She grasped the Hecatomb in frigid hands. "Chant your ritual words as I read ours. Night will end and life will again balance between Umbra and Lumina."

"I cannot. Archimage elders pass on the male canon orally." His head bowed. "Dag'ad did not teach me the words. I do not know the ritual."

Ana'hia stared a long time into the bowl, then set it back on the ice-skimmed stone.

"Do not know the ritual..." she whispered.

She gazed at the dark slash marking the cavern entrance and cried for wisdom that came too late.

C.S. Perryess

JACKSON'S PLAN

Sharp stabs of lightning bloodied the blue-black sky, throwing shadows and streaks and danger across the hunched backs of the laboring men. Their blue cotton work shirts were dark with rain and sweat. The shovels and picks in their hands swung rhythmically, the metal glinting in the silver flashes from above, as did the cold iron of the shackles linking them ankle to ankle.

They toiled, the mud sticky and thick in their boots. Even the full moon couldn't pierce those bullying clouds. Jackson stood and wiped his wide brown brow, looking out over the valley to the vulnerable little town in the vale. Jackson's determination doubled as his pick flew at a new pitch, recognizing the irrelevance of the car he had stolen back in '44, ten years ago, and those three dead boys, and the manslaughter conviction.

Blades of lightning played on Acton's glasses as he fought the sticky clay mud, scooping soggy shovelfuls up the embankment, as did Parsons, Hinejosa, Squeak, Barret and LaMonde, and further down the line of shackled men, Andrews and Bright, and Little Ben. The stubborn grating sound of pick and shovel on wet scree would have filled the air if the thunderclaps and downpour would have let up at all. The rain nearly screamed—its cry the never-ending scream of the violated, battering the men's ears like shrieks from a tortured past.

Of the fifteen inmates, Martens alone was free of the shackles. He pushed the wheelbarrow up and down a muddy, flowing rut as the others filled and emptied, filled and emptied. Martens' streaked and soaking shirt fit tightly around his giant arms and muscular back—his face and hands imperceptible in the black night. The thunder cracked and the huge man flinched—too much like the shotgun he had used on another long rainy night.

They slaved on. Like a precision machine they worked in the downpour—fifteen imperfect men and one imperfect cell block captain. The thunder rattled its chains, and on occasion each man looked down toward the quiet, vulnerable town, and up toward the hills, where the dam would soon burst -- up toward the lake and the prison, then higher still to the onslaught from the heavens.

Jackson's plan just might work. Maybe this huge trough, this banked pile of rock and rebar and mud, these seven and a half straight hours of labor, Barrett's pulled quad and Squeak's bloody foot would be worth it all. Maybe, right here where the canyon narrowed and branched, maybe this monumental last-minute effort would divert the waters from the defenseless town. Maybe LaMonde's wife, and Barrett's and Jackson's folks, Hinejosa's girl and Bright's little boy, maybe that volunteer who'd worked so hard with Squeak and Martens. Maybe the whole town would survive.

Captain Mayfield had been crazy to agree to this team—this group of men out at night—a wild night at that—but Mayfield also had kin in town, and he was as soaked, his muscles strained, working hard as the rest. He shoveled feverishly from ditch to barrow—thinking maybe Jackson's plan might work—maybe these men and their idea. Maybe.

Anne Schroeder

CANTINA NIGHTS

Esquival keeps an eye on the room.

Thirty years he has owned the cantina, both grown old now like his woman. Better for him that the *turistas* prefer the places with air conditioning because tonight will be long. Already he has filled a cardboard box with empty Tecate bottles.

At the bar an *Americano* sips Esquival's *pulque* from a clean glass. Ignoring the spate of Spanish behind him, he studies his hands with intensity that doesn't invite intrusion. His discolored leather sandals and baggy linen trousers have the look of a man who conducts business in Mexico with regularity. Perhaps he is an engineer searching for a mine, perhaps here in Casa Corte where cisterns collect stinking water the color of *pulque*, fit only for growing.

The heavy door creaks to admit a brace of cowboys, gringos before they speak, their Levis encrusted with dust from the road. Esquival watches without smiling as the smaller one claims the room even before the door swings shut. "Sheeeet…y'all burning trash in here?" This one will be the brawler. He wears a half-empty pack of Marlboros rolled high on his bicep, a sweat-stained straw hat shading his eyes, its brim rolled to a point in the front. Machismo.

While the locals pull their eyes to their *cervezas*, the two make a wide arc for a corner table. "Hey barkeep…we get brews over here?"

Esquival carries a pair of Coronas. Without expression plunks a half-dozen *limon* wedges on a pottery saucer before them.

Mendoza, a hard-eyed *mestizo* from Alamagorde taunts, "Heard you rich boys drink wine."

The brawler glares. His friend grins and toasts Mendoza with his bottle. "Sometimes, *amigo*, wine is like a woman. Good legs."

Mendoza doesn't let it go. "Maybe *Méjicano cerveza* puts hair on your *cojones*. That what you afraid of, pretty boy?" He snorts his derision.

Esquival glances from one to the other. It is the hour for trouble. Four against two, even if the locals hate Mendoza, they will fight and the gringos will lose. He tries diplomacy. "Both good for a thirsty man."

Mendoza tips back and squints into the chandelier. "Next time, you boys send your sisters down. We like the pretty girls to visit."

The room is still. Esquival has no hope that the gringos will settle into their drink before the question of insult occurs. The *Americano* watches also, too old for this bullshit, but not so much that he can't tell what is coming. An ally. Esquival bends close and forces lightness into his tone. "Hey, *amigo*...you ever have a woman sweet as tequila on a summer night?"

The *Americano* studies the bartender through the prism of his glass and nods. "I knew such a woman." The clinking bottles cease in the moment it takes him to decide. "I'll need another drink. Scotch. Women cause too much pain for *pulque*."

Esquival nods and pours. With any luck it will be a long story. They will get their money's worth. He closes his eyes.

Willy Bruijns

BYE

Now that people lived behind the new walls at the far end, the cow barn was Harry's favorite place. Sometimes he saw these people, a quick movement as they scurried back into their hiding place. Mom and Dad thought he didn't know but there was little on the farm that escaped his five-year old eyes and ears. Harry knew those people were Jews, even though to him they looked just like regular people.

Today Harry's brother Dirk was in the barn. Dirk was eighteen, as tall as Dad, and twice as strong. Dirk could toss Harry ten feet into the air and catch him as if he was no more than a newborn kitten. Not that Dirk noticed him much. Dirk was a man. He came and went as he pleased. He'd ride his bicycle to the village in plain view of the German soldiers and not be scared.

Dirk stood in the far corner but he wasn't alone. He had his arms around the waist of one of the girls who lived behind the walls. She twisted and pushed but Dirk held her tight. Harry knew that hold—once you're between those arms there was no escape.

Harry crept closer, hiding between two of the older heifers.

"Please don't," the girl said.

"It's like paying rent," Dirk said. "I'm here to collect."

Harry didn't know the Jews paid rent. He wondered how much.

"Please, no." She was crying.

Dirk turned her around and leaned her over the stall and then stared straight at where Harry stood between the cows.

Not knowing what to do, Harry put his hands on his head and twirled around. "Hey, look at me," he said.

"You stinking rat." Dirk lunged for him.

The girl ran back behind the wall.

It took a moment before Dirk's blow to his head started hurting, but Harry was already in full flight. He ran through the stalls, and would have made it out if he hadn't lost his footing when the last cow shifted. Dirk kicked him while the cows lowed in protest.

When Dirk stopped to catch his breath, Harry fled. He ran past the farmhouse down to the road where he sat and howled while examining his cuts and welts.

A truck with German soldiers drove by and stopped a few yards away. The driver, a blond German with a friendly face, called out "*Was ist los?*"

This was The Enemy. But they, too, looked like regular people. Friendly people.

"Nuffin'," Harry said, "Just my brother kissing a girl."

"A girl? His girlfriend, *ja?*"

"Nah, she don't wanna be his girlfriend. She lives in our barn."

Harry wondered why the man got out of the truck.

After the Germans rounded up the Jews and arrested Dad and Dirk, Harry stood by the kitchen door, his hand holding Mom's.

Out the back of the truck he saw the girl's tear-streaked face.

"Hey," Harry yelled.

The girl looked at him, lifted her hand, and mouthed, "Bye."

Susan Tuttle

FIGMENT

The police car squeals to a stop; officers race up the steps, through the doorway. I watch them bend over Andrew. The light in his eyes is dimming; scissors stick up from his chest. Not bad work for someone who's invisible.

A suited detective calls for an ambulance.

"Don't bother. He'll be dead before it gets here," I tell her. But she doesn't see or hear me.

I've been invisible for years. In the beforetime I was real, but Andrew ended that. Once the ring was on my finger, he denied me existence. At first, I was invisible only to him. Then other people started losing sight of me. Now, no one can see or hear me. It's an interesting way to live.

"She… she…" Andrew struggles. The detective bends lower.

"A woman did this?" she asks. Andrew nods. "Who?"

"My…wife," Andrew whispers. Then he dies.

"Canvas the neighborhood," the detective orders. "Find out what anyone heard, or saw. And find this wife!"

She walks over to the desk, to our wedding picture, searches for something more recent. She won't find it; the invisible don't photograph well. People come and leave, taking Andrew with them.

A patrolman tows in Andrew's friend, Mitch, and his wife, Sarah. Mourning, they extol his virtues. Naturally; Andrew was kind to everyone but me.

* * * *

Mitch frowns an answer. "He wasn't married."

"He didn't need to be," Sarah adds. "He was so… domestic on his own."

Right. If they only knew.

They look at the wedding picture and shake their heads, puzzled. They have never seen me. The detective thanks them and they leave. She again scrutinizes the scene, then turns to the window, almost bumping into me. She stops, frowns, peers in my direction. Then she blinks and shakes her head. She stares out the window until a sound in the hallway turns her around. She gasps, startled, and takes a step back.

"Who are you?" She looks at the blood on my hands. "The wife."

"You can see me?" I ask.

"Shouldn't I?"

"I'm invisible. At least, I used to be. Strange." I look at where Andrew fell. Did he recreate me by dying? It seems so, but I doubt he intended it.

The detective looks at the wedding picture. "You haven't changed much. Why did you kill him?"

"I didn't mean to," I say. "It was an experiment. I was trying to make him see me."

She gives me a look, half disgusted, half fascinated. "We searched the house. Where were you?"

I smile. "I've been here all along. Right beside you."

"Yeahhhh…" she says, rolling her eyes. "What a nutcase."

* * * *

She calls the uniforms. They handcuff me, put me in a squad car. But I've learned from Andrew. I bend my head and focus my mind.

One by one they will all wink out of existence. It's easy; if you don't give control to someone else, you can create your own reality. Invisible or not.

Joe Amaral

MANKIND

I forge ahead heedlessly, blind to the warnings. Everybody tells me to turn around—the animals, plants, and sentient beings, while they continue to run the opposite way. I am a wildfire ripping through the landscape in destructive fury. Slash and burn, use and usurp. God throws javelin bolts of lightning to blaze my path; in His name I charge.

I can't care less.

First they try to subtly deter me. Beavers gnaw down trees to block my path. They divert and widen streams to prevent my crossing. I can't walk on water, but I can build a bridge that will. I out-dam them as well, damning us all. My chainsaw roars, reaming nature's stillness. They cower fearfully in their hovels. Rivers of teardrops spray my burlap face. The cries of dehydrated waterways reverberate in my thick skull.

Stoic sylvans chatter angrily from root holes. Sylvans are silly creatures I spit upon, stick figures of ancient magic and faerie dust, their tatty wisps of powers long since forgotten. No one believes in fantasy anymore, science ruthlessly wrested control of this land.

The iron grip of fact trumps wishful fiction. They pelt me with small objects, or whatever projectiles they get their knobby wooden stumps around to fling. Talons and claws reach out to rake me off the trail. Tree branches lurch and widow-makers fall. I tear through their kamikaze dive bombs.

The lion and wolf packs give me quite the alarming ambush, grunting in prideful harrumphs of attack. Their moves are too antiquated, and my evolution too profound to be fooled by their traps. Hunting is simply a baby game of tag-you're-it, duck-duck-goose, or mushroom-in-the-middle. The chase became tiresome. I am not the prey. I am the assassin.

Adjustments must be made when a world is dying. Some species don't have adequate time or resolve to genetically alter inbred habits. Some adapt faster, survive longer. The delay isn't worth it. Inevitably, even the best prepared get caught, as malleable time slowly hardens to culmination.

Untamed pit bulls have been patiently waiting for this moment, their dead-eyed detachment staring me down, deciding whether to lick or lacerate me. I admire their shark-like voracity. Their ancestral grit fakes docile domestication, embers of wilderness survival still residing beneath, inextinguishable by master man.

Housebroken humans are yammering lapdogs now, beyond yearning the wolf's cry. We're simply shattered shells, empty of echoes.

Echo.

We are what we are I reckon. Or were.

(Sigh)

Who's next?

Angels whisper insidiously, casting brilliant light to blind my eyes. I find it quite demonic; their halos encircling me like handcuffs. I brush searing rings off my scalp, childish heavenly glitter, though their hymns linger like fiery cobwebs. Angels are tricky beings, and don't like to get dirty wearing all that white. Most have fallen darkly into oblivion anyhow. Religion is a fairy tale. I use crutches as weapons. I don't lean on them.

A wraith named Love keeps stalking me, reminding my subconscious of past hurts. She is hard to elude despite my best efforts. The odiferous crescendo of crumpled T-shirts and castaway memories, old scents triggering tidal failures. Love rips the cord of remembrance mercilessly. I constantly work to repel this sad nostalgia in my mind; it's what brought me to this imminent future. I learn to live with it, though the pieces she steals add up exponentially. She tantalizes my senses agog.

So I turn my nose and blow.

I am the wings that make the winds rage—a turbine of terror, a predatory propeller.

I cavitate the beauty of birdsong.

The waterfalls are dying, you are killing them, they lyrically twitter.

Extinction is to be expected, I coldly reply.

The curtain holding the sky together rips ominously. I cannot meet the gaze of death, the emptiness awaiting. Head down I charge into billowing black robes and skeletal caresses.

I peak but keep climbing. I stand atop the world rind, peeling the soft bare skin of Earth to her glowing core. Her magma bubbles in my hand. My blood boils. I sow the soil waterless, stripping it of minerals. The molten coals are my eyes as lava flows quench my greedy thirst. Filled with lust, I drink until they become smoldering ash, petrified, frozen in fear. Cold rock is all that remains, the basalt of bereaved atrocities committed. Seduction is a smokeless enigma.

I am mankind.

The only living things left standing are my fellow parasites. Eternally patient, they follow to feast on the chaos, on the carcasses I leave in my wake. Humanity will trip up soon. I am slowly killing myself.

They wait to feast on me.

Donna Reese

LULL

A zippity–do–da blue sky right out of a 40's musical, color by Technicolor. In the west, though, clouds with attitude assemble and cha cha towards us. It's April's jest, just messing with our heads between spring storms. We are giddy and don't give a damn that the daffodils nodding their necks coyly are really not more golden and gorgeous this year. We don't care that dew drops on bare branches looking like diamonds on a necklace was always a cliché; it's brilliant. It's poetry. But, we have no time. New storm clouds have stepped up their pace. Lulls are on the clock and the window on our euphoria is closing.

Turning back to my walk, I see a hiker approaching. She's not plugged into anything, my usual excuse for avoiding pleasantries. We nod the walkers' nod. She almost passes, but not quite. We are so close our elbows might have touched. She hesitates, "Isn't it a gorgeous day?" and passes near me. Then a groan and stumble. I pivot and catch her elbow before she hits the dirt.

"That was close," I say. She does not respond, seems shaken, hangs on. Maybe twisted something. "Can you make it to that bench? Just lean on me."

She nods and I guide us to the still wet bench. We sit. She is crying. "Did you hurt yourself?"

She shakes her head, tries to straighten, to speak. "Maybe it would be better if you just cry." I hear a softness in my tone, pull out a damp tissue from my jeans, put it into her hand.

"Not yet." Her voice is tight. "I can't yet." She begins to talk. "I have a son. He is very ill. Leukemia." She wads the tissue beyond use. "He won't get well."

I look around, for a way out, but hear myself say, "Tell me about your son. What's his name?"

"Charlie. He's called Charlie." At the sound of his name, I feel her relax against me, her fingers releasing the tissue. "He's seven and really starting to grow up, put his little red wagon in the garage last fall. Now it's baseball. Cards, mitts, caps, bats. Anything baseball. We were just changing out the trains he used to love…"

As she relives Charlie's life before his illness, all I see is the enamel basin, cloudy juice glass with its bent straw, pill bottles crowding the comic books to the edge of the night table. A tide of medical stuff pushing childhood into the corner, onto the shelf next to the baseball mitt, the Paddington bear. Not room enough for everything.

It's a story I've heard before, tried not to read in some magazine, no more new than the yellowness of daffodils, the lull between storms. The words I say to her are not new. "If there is anything I can do . . ." knowing there is not. We both know, sitting on that park bench, the dampness wicking up through our clothes, living out the clichés of our lives. Our elbows touch.

Shirley Powell

THE IN GROUP

The only rule was that you couldn't tell. I had wanted to be part of that "in" group so bad I didn't think twice. "I promise," I said.

Dana smiled. "Prove it."

The girls leaned forward.

Dana opened a purple pouch and withdrew a silver scalpel. "Hold out your arm."

My stomach tightened. "What are you doing?"

"No wusses in this club. Christ! We all did it."

Dana turned my arm over. Before I could object, she swiftly drew the knife down my arm. Gasps, oohs, and sighs erupted from the admiring audience. I watched, fascinated, as a line of blood bloomed on my white forearm.

"Okay. You're in. Cutting's the first secret."

I pressed Kleenex on my arm as we sprawled on deep carpet scattered with oversized pillows. Her parents were on a cruise. "They trust me because I get good grades. I'm mature for sixteen and have nice, responsible friends." They laughed and punched pillows. My parents trust me, too, I thought remorsefully.

Dana lit a scented candle, placed it on the floor, and motioned us closer. From a leather pouch she withdrew a joint, lit it from the candle and passed it around.

She intoned, "This meeting will now come to order."

Laughter, screams, and more pillow-punching followed.

She pointed to Madison. "You. Did you follow orders? Show us."

Madison removed a black velvet box from her purse.

"Open it."

Madison opened the case and raised a green carved necklace.

"Where'd you get it?" Dana demanded.

"Neiman Marcus."

"That's not a Neiman Marcus box."

"Well I couldn't ask for a box, could I?"

More laughter.

"What's next? Ideas? C'mon."

"iPhone," someone shouted.

Nodding, she pointed to me. "Bring an iPhone to the next meeting."

"But I can't afford one."

"Stupid. You're supposed to lift it. To make sure you do, I'll go along. Just this first time."

In the crowded store, I held a pink iPhone, touching buttons, asking questions. The clerk said," Wait a second," and turned toward another customer.

"Now," whispered Dana. Holding the iPhone down by my thigh I began to leave, my heart thumping, when the clerk suddenly asked me for it. Dana slipped the iPhone from my hand.

"I put it on the counter," I said. Out of nowhere, a man wearing a security badge appeared. "Follow me."

"Are you accusing us of shoplifting?" Dana asked, awkwardly bumping into a man wearing cargo pants. "My parents'll sue your ass."

We had to empty our purses and pockets on a desk. Clean. Suddenly a siren blared. Mr. Cargo Pants stood outside the door looking bewildered. "I don't know how that got in my pocket."

"Yeah, we've heard that one."

"I didn't steal anything. Take your hands off me!"

He pulled away. The policeman forced him to the ground.

Ignoring his protests, Dana swished past. I was paralyzed. "You coming with me or not?" she called over her shoulder.

"Excuse me," I said to the officer. "I have something to tell you."

Willy Bruijns

CROSSROADS

They gazed at the flat expanse all around them. The midday sun beamed down, the two of them casting the only shadow as far as he could see.

"Do you live around here?" he asked.

"God no," she said, making a face. "Do you?"

"Me? No. No, no, no," he lied. "No, not me."

"Visiting family?" she asked.

"Friends."

"Me too."

The Greyhound bus had dropped them off a moment ago and then had moved on, leaving a trace of dust far away, the rumble of its engine now reduced to a hum hardly audible above the buzzing of crickets and cicadas.

He couldn't remember ever before getting off the bus with another passenger. It had surprised him to find he had company standing here at the crossroads.

"Is someone picking you up?" she asked.

"No, I'll walk."

She looked around. "How can you tell which way to go?"

He laughed, as if she had said something witty.

"No, really," she said.

He shrugged. "I've been here before. I know which way to go."

He saw her look him up and down, saw her notice his surplus army boots and short hair.

"You in the army?" she asked.

"Just finished." Another lie.

"Did they send you anywhere? Iraq or Afghanistan?"

"No, I guess I was lucky."

"You were," she said.

She looked pretty with her long black hair, her black and white checkered shirt and her faded blue jeans. Her boots were simple, but made from soft tan leather. City boots. She carried a large duffel bag made of the same leather.

"Are you staying long?" he asked.

"Just for the weekend."

They looked away, surveying the vast nothingness of the New Mexico plane.

"Do you want me to wait with you?"

"Wait for what?" she said.

"Your ride, your friends," he said, "whoever will be picking you up."

"No, thanks. Who knows how long that'll take." She put her duffel bag down.

"Oh. Okay." He wanted to stay with her a while longer. "Well, enjoy your weekend," he said and turned to go.

"You too."

He walked in the direction of his home. After a few minutes he turned and waved. She waved back.

He walked on, towards the slight depression that hid the village. Where he used to live in a trailer with his dad and too many brothers and sisters. There at the end of the dirt road, where a seasonal stream allowed the only few trees for miles around. Where for so long his parents had told him he'd grow up to be no good, that it finally had come true.

He hadn't been home for three months, doing time for drunk driving. Drunk driving without a license. Drunk driving without a license that had been suspended the previous time he'd been drunk. Now he walked back home to boredom, to drinking beer and shooting at empties.

He turned again to look at the young woman at the crossroads. She was looking in the direction of a faraway plume of dust, which was making its way toward her.

He dropped his bag and ran. He got to her out of breath, but before the car had reached her.

"When are you taking the bus back?" he asked.

"Monday," she smiled. "Whatever time the bus gets here. Around nine, I think?"

"Me too," he said and smiled back at her.

He reached out his hand. "Antone."

She put her hand into his. "Ella," she said. "Nice to meet you, Antone."

"And you, Ella."

The car had reached the crossroads. A young couple got out.

"Ella!" The woman hugged her friend. "You made it. Welcome to our new world."

Ella introduced the couple to him. "They've just moved here," she said. "They're building a home."

Antone nodded in greeting. He was relieved that these were strangers, newcomers, people who didn't know him.

"Why here?" he asked.

"We wanted to go to a place where things are simpler," the woman said.

Antone nodded.

"I'll see you Monday," he said to Ella, and with a wave of his hands he turned in the direction of his home, which he would leave for good on Monday. Leave it to seek his way out of the boredom that Ella's friends had termed the simpler life. Perhaps he'd get to know Ella. Perhaps she'd become his friend. Perhaps he'd travel to where she lived. And perhaps he'd catch up to his lies, and become just a visitor to this barren plane, or even join the army until he knew where to go next.

Anna Unkovich

GIFT FROM AN ACHING HEART

I listened to the slamming of the kitchen door and the unmistakable reverberation of the suitcase wheels *ka-plunk, ka-plunk, ka-plunking* across the tile floor. Soon to follow was the more muted *ker-plop, ker-plop, ker-plopping* of this vessel rolling across the carpeting. It was not the first time that I had heard these sounds.

I said nothing, but followed her into the bedroom and sat on the edge of the bed trying to make eye contact—to elicit guilt. Helpless, I watched the details of her packing; the way she carefully folded each item, placing it into a Ziploc bag for protection, the way she packed small items into shoes, or into corners to fill the spaces.

I loved watching every move she made. I loved the gentle touch of her hand when she was pleased with me. I loved the smell of her favorite coconut lotion that she said reminded her of Hawaii. Simply being in the same room with her was a blessing.

Now she was leaving, unaware of the depths of my feelings. For seven years I had trusted her with my love—all of it. I had been faithful, without a single stray moment. Oh, I may have briefly looked to others for attention. But it was only that—attention. There was no love involved. And, it only happened when she was too busy with her work to spend time with me.

I could never tell her how I felt. Instead, I lavished gifts upon her—daily gifts, too precious for words. I thought of the moments when we gazed into each other's eyes with unspoken adoration. I thought of lying with our bodies so close that our hearts beat almost as one. Must love always be professed in its loudest notes?

I heard a sound much like a baby wailing, and realized that it was coming from my own throat. I was ashamed, even embarrassed, at its begging tone. I craved one last touch from her.

I followed her to the door, pausing momentarily for a violent, retching cough. We both knew it was nothing for concern. It was a chronic condition that would not halt her departure.

With the closing of the door, I plotted my revenge on my way back to the room and the bed that we shared. Lying on her side of the bed, I burrowed my face into her pillow, drowning myself in the remaining scent of her. Feeling the expensive satin and lace against my face, I already missed her beyond measure. She owned only the best, and I once felt honored to be among her chosen possessions.

Another round of retching overtook me. Then another. Finally, I purged the large, slimy fur ball onto her pillow. It did not ease my aching heart, but it would be a small gift for her upon her return from yet one more business trip.

Willy Bruijns

BEST FRIENDS

When your dad doesn't answer your knock on his bedroom door, even though you know he is in there with someone, because you heard his familiar gritty rumble of a voice, and that someone's light, flirty giggle, when those voices stop and then whisper with urgency after you wiggle the handle of the *locked door* and call out "Dad?", you run to the kitchen and take out a toothpick because the lock on that door is one of those bathroom locks, a poke through that hole and the locking lever pops up, the door opens and here he is in bed with someone hiding under the red flowered duvet you picked out with your mom when she was still alive, but you already recognized the voice and know who it is from the best friend bracelet on the nightstand *on your mother's side.*

It's Trisha.

Trisha with your dad.

In the middle of the day when you were supposed to be swimming except you got your period.

Trisha with whom you grew up, being next door neighbors only five years apart, Trish now twenty, and you too young to be in bed with anyone let alone someone's dad, although perhaps you should have guessed from the last few months, Trish asking if your dad was dating yet, it had been a year since your mom, well, you know, and then saying that your dad was hot, "yeah right" you said, and Trish said "Word, Amanda, word" trying to be hood-ish while shopping at Victoria's Secrets for new bras and matching thongs, ignoring your protest that you wouldn't pay *twenty-five dollars* for anything that small, even if it was the only thing you could wear with skinny jeans, and then Trish looking at you so serious and saying you had to be prepared for when it happened.

Happened?

"You know," she said, "When you meet someone and have sex."

Sex, the logical next step now that your body has gone from bony to curvy, now that you have breasts, even if they aren't as round and big as Trish's, now that boys *see* you but especially Trish, with her long hair, curly like a gypsy, and the nonchalant effect of her carefully selected flimsy flannel shirt, almost see-through, tied in a knot around her waist so that the flesh of her hips sways naked over the top of jeans that end in the fuzz of brown Uggs and make you wish you could dress like that.

But your dad frowned on anything too showy and you never want to disappoint him.

Disappoint him, hah!

"Christ, Amanda," your dad says, his arm around the lump that is your best friend for life, Trisha, his eyes pleading.

You slam the door, and scream "*But you're my….*" and the words *dad* and *best friend* clash in mid-air and evaporate in the boiling bubbles of your sobs.

Anne R. Allen

AUNT DOREEN'S LEGACY

My cousin Veronica still talked with her mouth full.

"It's so tragic that Aunt Doreen died here all alone," she said as the cookie crumbs fell down the front of her black funeral outfit.

I agreed it was sad. Aunt Doreen didn't seem to have had a lot of friends. Except for a few Stratford Cosmetics sales ladies, nobody but family had showed up for her memorial service.

"I like that scent you're wearing," Veronica said. I knew she was trying to make nice, but it was kind of pushy how she sniffed my neck, like we were still ten-year-old best buddies. It had been a decade since we'd even exchanged a Christmas card. "It's way nicer than that god-awful Stratford perfume Aunt Doreen used to give you." She gave a phony laugh. "What was it called? 'Night Won't Fall,' 'Night Must Fall,' Night… something."

"*Nightwood's Call* was the name." I grabbed the last chocolate chip cookie as the Stratford ladies vultured around Aunt Doreen's battered dining table. "Aunt Doreen decided it was my 'signature scent.' It smelled like it could kill cockroaches."

We should have been grieving, but I just felt weird and numb. It's always sad when somebody dies, but Aunt Doreen was pretty old, and she'd never had a relationship with us kids—except to send us that tacky perfume at holidays and birthdays.

"At least yours came in a cool purple bottle." Veronica was still talking to me, but her focus was on Aunt Doreen's knick-knack shelves. She was scoping them out like an early bird at a garage sale. "The perfume she chose for me came in a jar shaped like big, pink lips: *Kiss Me Quick*. It smelled like bubble gum." She opened the doors to the china cabinet. "Nothing here but these stupid sales awards." She counted the plastic trophies. "She was the district's top seller for…what, twenty years? Where did it go? She never spent a dime, from the looks of this dump. She must have saved up quite a nest egg."

Okay, Veronica was cutting to the chase. The two of us had inherited Aunt Doreen's estate, which didn't appear to be much. But the family always suspected there was more.

"That old girl's got loot hidden away," Mom used to say. "Probably stashed in that cellar." Aunt Doreen kept a big padlock on the cellar door and never let anybody go down there.

As if she'd been reading my mind, Veronica pulled a key ring from her pocket. "I found these in the desk. One's gotta get us into that cellar. Wanna check it out?"

It seemed tacky to disappear in the middle of the funeral reception, but I wasn't going to let Veronica snoop around without me.

We finally got the rusty lock open, and I flicked on my purse flashlight as Veronica led the way down some creaky old stairs. I could barely breathe—the place had the strangest smell.

"What do you think we're looking for?" Veronica said. "Piles of stocks and bonds? Jars of coins, put up like canned peaches?"

I beamed the flashlight around the dirt-floor room, which was lined with rows of shelves, crammed with stuff. Not jars or stock certificates. Something papery and pink: Stratford Cosmetics bags— all full. Hundreds of them. Veronica pulled one out, still stapled with an invoice. Never opened. No customer name.

We realized the truth at the same moment.

"Oh, my god," Veronica said. "She bought all this…herself?"

"One way to be district seller of the year." I felt a little sick.

Veronica ripped open a bag and pulled out a jar shaped like big fuchsia lips. It stank of rotten bubble gum. She pulled out another—Raid-scented and purple. "Here," she said, with a catch in her voice. "Your legacy. *Nightwood's Call.*"

She grabbed me in a hug and my own eyes stung—as I felt real grief for our Aunt Doreen.

FOR EVERY READING TASTE

Anne Peterson

AHOY, CRIPPLES!

Well, technically I'm a cripple. They don't call us that now. But my mind dances, my spirit cartwheels. Even at my most exuberant, though, I didn't picture myself as a mermaid, sharing a tropical lagoon with manatees. But thanks to Ramon, it happened. I'd been painfully arthritic for about ten years when I fell in love with Ramon, an inventive scapegrace who didn't let the limp caused by his worn-out total hip replacement get in the way of living. He played the guitar with passion and vibrated with ideas.

Ramon figured exercise was critically important to both of us, but he didn't want "this up-down, up-down weight-lifting," he said. "I want exercise as my lifestyle, part of everyday behavior."

A sailing enthusiast, Ramon didn't take long to hatch a picturesque plot. We'd pool our meager incomes, buy a small sailboat, and live where the water was warm enough for year-round swimming. We'd live afloat, getting exercise sailing, rowing a dinghy, and snorkeling daily. The weather, he predicted, would be so hot in such a place that we'd be forced to cool off by flopping off the side of the boat into the water, exerting our disabled limbs without putting weight on them.

We cast around for such a situation and came up with the Florida Keys, a necklace of one hundred islands strung on US Highway 1 from Key Largo to Key West. The water surrounding the Keys is very shallow and warm on the Bay side, deeper and slightly less warm on the Atlantic side. Coral reefs, tropical fish, and "gin-clear water" (as locals said), would add sublime beauty to daily exercise. Countless coves and mangrove islands abounded for shelter.

Since water on the Bay side is ten feet deep max, it should be possible to throw out an anchor almost anywhere. The way Ramon figured, we should be able to live in Paradise, getting everything we needed for body and soul. And not even have mortgage payments or rent. A crazy idea, you say?

But that was our life for twenty years. We took sabbaticals for joint replacements for one or the other of us, but our normal life was unimaginably free and beautiful, with meaningful exercise all the time. Living in nature without benefit of electricity, plumbing, or the normal conveniences was difficult, but we toughened up and enjoyed the hardship, for it meant self-reliance and peace. It was do-able. We were active and healthy.

I missed writing on my electric typewriter (those were pre-computer days), but couldn't have managed it anyway. My hands and wrists had become too painful. What I was driven to do, since I felt compelled to write no matter what, was painstakingly hand-letter everything on good days. It was terribly tedious, but then, I was terribly compulsive. I sent off articles to boating magazines, amazed when they were accepted, although the format certainly wasn't standard. I sold several articles with my illustrations to local publications, too. It was satisfying.

We loved the life. We knew where the scallops migrated every year and dived up many feasts' worth. We hobnobbed with manatees, not in an aquarium, but in the lagoons where they lived. We got so friendly they let me stuff lettuce into their mouths. We discovered where the brilliantly colored exotic fish hung out, and we did, too. We soaked in the medicinal acids around mangrove roots in water dark as coffee.

We thrilled at the brilliant summer sunsets whose crimson glow tinted the sea's surface the color of burgundy. In that water world where only a mile-wide strip of islands separated east from west, we watched spectacular sunrises, protected our skin from noontime scorch, and then welcomed the dazzle of sunsets. Sometimes at night phosphorescent shapes and sparks revealed movements of fish, a breathtaking wonder. Even our own splashes glowed. It was all accompanied by classical guitar music.

And we sailed. Ramon, non-mechanical as he was, refused to tolerate a dirty, complicated motor. It was a challenge to sail against wind and tide; getting through drawbridges without catastrophe was a real accomplishment. Ramon was known locally as either a consummate sailor or a total lunatic. He was both.

My writer's heart was loaded with impressions, experiences, stories, and material. It was great therapy while it lasted, and it lasted longer than we dared to expect. Now it lives only in the memories of Ramon, me, and my computer. But it worked!

Dennis Eamon Young
LAST CALL

He was dead tired; it had been a long day at the store. Ryan had built new displays the entire time, so he would have extra money for Gloria's visit. Everything had to be just right—the house fixed up—even a banner proclaiming, "Welcome Gloria." He was in a hurry to get to the airport, to be there for the call telling him her flight had landed. Ryan planned to wrap her in the warmth of his waiting arms and never let her go; he'd been a fool to let her leave the first time.

From across the country and the intervening years, she'd suddenly promised to step back into his life. They had re-established that old bond of trust. Who said there were no second chances in life? He would use this visit to erase any lingering doubts she might have.

They had been a golden couple back then in New York. They were at the top of everyone's invitation list, dancing their way from one side of the city to the other. Friends enjoyed sharing in the easy glow of their love. They just hadn't been ready to settle down, so they followed separate dreams.

Ryan had the top down on the Eclipse to catch the cool night air in his unruly hair and keep him awake. He slid around the curvy nighttime roads he knew like a lover, roads meant for slower speeds. He was alive with the rush of adrenaline. He thought of how Gloria would enjoy driving these lovely roads with him. They would share the perfume of spring, the embracing warmth of summer, and the shimmering colors of fall as they wound their way through the countryside.

"Damn," Ryan shouted, as he careened around a long curve, his eyes focused on the taillights of some slowpoke ahead. *Don't get excited.* There was a passing lane ahead; he could wait to pass legally.

He pulled into the outside lane as the two cars arrived at the passing markers. The other car sped up. Ryan caught up at the end of the passing lane, just in time to brake. His nemesis slowed down to a crawl. Again.

The scenario repeated itself over and over until Ryan's temper started to boil. They were approaching a long passing section leading to another turn. He knew he could pass this idiot before the curve. Even if he wasn't back in his lane, he could see oncoming traffic by watching for headlights through the trees.

As the two cars cruised around the turn, the other car shot ahead with Ryan in hot pursuit, rational thought left behind. A little more than halfway through the section, Ryan saw the curve at the end. *No headlights coming toward me.* He pulled into the outside lane, increased his speed and closed the distance between him and the mystery car.

With about ten feet between them, the other car swerved out in front of Ryan and braked. Ryan stomped on his own brakes to avoid a collision and the other car took off again. With a sickening feeling, Ryan felt his rear tires slip and slide to the left. Years of driving experience kept him calm. Time slowed while he fought to regain control.

The Eclipse entered the turn sliding sideways, hit the guardrail broadside and facing the wrong way. Still fighting for control, Ryan swung the car away from the rail. Momentum carried it around, and it hit the guardrail again, this time facing in the right direction, but losing its fight with gravity. The Eclipse flipped over the railing and sailed out over the embankment toward the murmuring creek below. The battered sports car landed top-down in the arms of two old trees. Ryan's cell phone rang as his broken body hung in his seatbelt.

As his life ebbed away, he opened the phone and took his last call: it was Gloria, but he hadn't the strength left to speak.

"Ryan, are you there?" she said in her soft, sweet voice. "I'm sorry. I'm not coming. I've found someone else."

Debby Nicklas

AN OLD DOG

Everyone loves a puppy but it is an old dog which lingers in our hearts. The puppy eyes have grown tired, yet are filled with the wisdom of an old soul. The colorful fur around the face has turned gray. The young body now limps and creaks slowly around the house with never any indication of pain or sorrow.

Our dog is thirteen years old. It's hard to imagine her as a puppy or even in her middle years when she was strong and vibrant. But the spirit of that dog is still found in her eyes. Those eyes show love, kindness, acceptance, and loyalty. It is as if the younger version of her is trapped in this old body. Her presence is a reminder of the best way to honor the cycle of life—how we are born with a sense of joy and adventure and then grow old with dignity and an acceptance of a life well-lived.

I will always remember the day we met our yellow Lab, Sunny, for the first time. She was the gentle one in the litter. My husband wanted the bigger one. My younger son, Jeff, wanted the more playful one. It was Danny, my older son's choice since it was his birthday present. Always insightful, he was set on the quiet one and we never looked back. Sunny would be our family dog. We all fell in love with her.

It is odd, though, that today what I recall most is not all the wonderful memories of the day to day life with a dog, but how her sleeping spots over these thirteen years have reflected the many stages of our family's life.

Our new puppy slept in a crate in Danny's room. The crate was used for house-training purposes. For my son, it was a time to learn responsibility for the caring of another living being. However, the caring went both ways. Many of our photos show Sunny and Danny sleeping together on his bed, both content and filled with the promise of another tomorrow. Then, a few years later, when Danny was older and did not need the warmth and comfort at night, Sunny began to sleep in my younger son's room, as if she knew that it was his time for support during the dark nights of childhood dreams and nightmares.

As the years passed and our boys grew up, the sleeping arrangements continued to change as well. Our dog found the comfort of a big red chair in the living room. Though Sunny knew the rule was no dogs on the furniture, at night she would climb up as if she was guarding the house for all of us sleeping upstairs. She loved that chair and we did not have the heart to discipline her, so we lived with the dog hair.

Then as Sunny grew older and it became harder to climb, she would settle at the bottom of the staircase near the front door, just waiting for the boys to come home from their late nights with friends or summer jobs. Today, at age thirteen, climbing to that first landing on the stairs is too difficult for her; she stays on the living room floor. The boys are away at college and graduate school now, but her nighttime ritual of lying close to the front door persists. I believe she is still waiting for them to come home.

It is sad to know that Sunny will never climb those stairs again to sleep in our bedrooms and guard us in our rooms. However, her presence in the house remains special and important. Looking into her eyes, I see how much protection, love, and devotion our dog has given our family. I draw comfort in knowing that Sunny was also protected, loved and cared for by all of us.

So these days our roles have reversed. Often, we will sleep downstairs in our guest bedroom just to be near her in case she needs the comfort and support that she has given us over these many years.

An old dog is a most precious gift.

Judith Bernstein

TO KINDLE OR NOT TO KINDLE

Books are the entryway to new friendships, to love, to adventure, to family history—the possibilities are endless. Kindles are efficient, cost effective, and of course, the latest in book technology. Which to buy and for what reason, that is the question. What follows is a biased view of books in print with some balance added by friends who are ardent e-book fans.

Let's consider the book. Although you may not be able to judge a book by its cover, you might judge a potential mate by his or her books. During my dating days, I often scrutinized a date's bookshelf. Was there an overlap between my taste for poetry and science fiction and his books? Even if we had nothing bookish in common, I could at least open a conversation by saying: "So, what did you think of Ken Kesey's, *One Flew over the Cuckoo's Nest?* These days, if my date was a Kindle-user, I would have to peruse his downloads and that isn't a task that can be done surreptitiously.

Books can be beautiful, decorative, and a way of asserting one's taste, hence the hefty coffee-table book. On my table, I proudly display a book about the artist, Georgia O'Keefe, complete with gorgeous color plates of her paintings and a book about Oregon's wild rivers. I offer friends a chance to leaf through them while I am cooking or on the phone. I suppose a book can be left open on the table but somehow this seems an unlikely scenario.

And what about those chance conversations struck up at a doctor's office, on a bus, or in a cafe because someone was reading one of your favorite books? On the other hand, it's hard to see what's on someone's Kindle; it seems more an invasion of privacy to sneak a look over a shoulder than to spot a book jacket across a crowded room.

I like to read to kids and appreciate creative pop-up children's books. No matter how deep the colors and how well-lit the screen, a two dimensional object is not the same as a three-dimensional book. And then there's the economic angle. The Kindle cannot be chained to my beach towel and might be stolen, but if someone grabs my used paperback beach read, who cares? So there are tactile and monetary advantages to a book.

Books remind us of our personal history. The sight of a book read in childhood or at a critical time in one's life can bring a wave of memories like Proust's flood of same upon tasting a Madeleine. A book, like a cookie, may bring "*Remembrance of Things Past.*" I recently packed for a move and discovered a copy of a college favorite, James Joyce's, *Portrait of the Artist as a Young Man.* Seeing it brought back memories of the professor who taught the class and the friends who were part of my life at that time.

Children can learn family history, even its secrets, by discovering books on a shelf that belonged to their mother, grandmother, or even a great grandfather. The book might have a message or inscription, and a date written on the front page, or have food stains on it. It might smell old. They reach for the book, open it, and begin to ask questions. Books are a gateway to history in a way that a Kindle download is not.

Let's consider the Kindle or other ways of accessing e-books. Price is a big plus, as is portability. Setting out on a long journey, who wants to haul five or six books when a Kindle is lighter and affords the opportunity to read as many books as one likes. The ability to change fonts and type size is especially advantageous for middle-age nearsightedness. And increasingly, Kindles are used for reading far more than books: magazines, journal article reprints, and of course, internet access, all in one tidy bundle. Finally, there are "books" that will never see the printed page, available only as a download.

Naturally, there are pluses and minuses to both e-books and print books; the trick is to learn the virtues of each. To rephrase historical advice: Render unto Kindle the things that are Kindle's and unto books, the things that are books.

Willy Bruijns

DUSK

Rosemarie picks up her purple sweater and tries to remember how to fold it. Such an easy thing, she's done it her whole life. But as she holds up the sweater she can't recall how.

Her suitcase is open on her bed. She's packing to go somewhere. But where? She closes her eyes, balls her fists and squeezes her eyebrows together in the effort to remember.

Nothing.

She'll ask Tom. He'll know, he always does.

She opens her mouth to the word "Tom"—but remembers just then that Tom is no longer around. It is why she's packing. To go away.

To move to another place.

A home.

"Mom?" The voice from behind startles Rosemarie. She is no longer certain about who people are, or why they're here, and a surge of panic makes her twitch.

"It's me, Mom. Evelyn?" The voice is hesitant, but the hand that touches Rosemarie's shoulder is gentle.

Evelyn. Her daughter.

Rosemarie remembers her daughter. The girl with reading glasses too big for her face. First in her class. Such a serious little girl, always worried, always fretting over problems that didn't exist. But sweet and smart and pretty in her own freckled way.

Rosemarie turns, still holding the sweater, expecting to see an eight-year-old girl with braids and glasses, and sees a woman in her fifties.

The woman takes the sweater. "You still have that? Remember when Dad bought you that sweater? You were surprised he bought something you actually liked. Remember?"

Rosemarie nods, but doesn't remember. She watches the woman fold the sweater with an easy move and put it in the suitcase.

She says, "Is Tom packed?" and looks in the woman's face for remnants of that young freckled girl.

The woman's bright smile falters, "Oh Mom," she says and puts her arms around Rosemarie's shoulders. "Dad's gone, remember? He died. End of last year."

Dang it, she knew that. SHE KNEW THAT! She is so mad at herself she wants to hit something, throw something, somehow hurt someone. She digs her nails into her palms to keep from screaming out loud. Why can't she hang on to what she knows? Her thoughts are like floating soap bubbles. She never knows where they go or when they pop. She can't control them, can't hang on to them. Not even with the most strenuous effort.

Her nails leave a series of purple indentations on hands that look foreign to her. So wrinkled and dry. Thin, yellow skin over blue veined flesh. Are these her own hands? How did they get so old?

Rosemarie looks at her suitcase and realizes that once she closes the front door behind her, her past will dim even more. She'll be surrounded by the darkness of yesterday and the uncertainty of a future she can't grasp any longer. Tomorrow she'll be lost forever.

She sits on the edge of her bed. Sorrow, starting in her stomach, moves up through her body in sobbing heaves until it burns tears through her eyes, releasing the pressure that threatens to explode her head.

She'll be leaving her house, the last place that is familiar. The only place where she can wake up and know where she is. While the outside world has become a mystery, inside she still knows where the bathroom is, or how to get dressed—even if buttons and zippers have become a challenge. How can she leave the only place in the world where she can still find pieces of herself?

The woman who is her daughter sits down next to her, hugs her, her face caressing Rosemarie's like a cat. She feels tears on her daughter's face, feels her sadness as if she, too, is stranded on the island of now.

"Oh, honey," Rosemarie says.

"It'll be fine, Mom. You'll see. You'll like the place."

Rosemarie frowns. What place?

"Remember how much you like the gardens? And the staff is so nice. You'll see, you'll have a wonderful time there. So, stop worrying."

Rosemarie tries to remember a garden. She wipes her tears and wonders why she was crying. What gardens? She needs to pack. She's going on a trip somewhere. She needs her large brimmed straw hat for those gardens. And she'd better find Tom and help him pack. He's so forgetful these days.

Linda Mills

THE BEST TIME OF MY LIFE

Sometimes bad things happen for a good reason. Born nearly blind, I have learned the truth of that maxim during my 70 years. It really was my first thought that day in June, 2012 when the doctor told me I had tumors on both my kidneys. My husband had taken me to the hospital emergency room, suffering what turned out to be my first and, I am happy to say, my last gallbladder attack. A subsequent Sonogram verified the presence of the offending organ packed tight with gallstones. But it also showed a tennis ball-sized tumor on my right kidney and a golf ball-sized tumor on the left kidney. When the doctor broke the news it didn't come as a total surprise.

People are not always aware of how much information they telegraph through their body movements and muscle tension. I can't see faces but I can sense what my contemporaries would call "bad vibes." After a few minutes of the Sonogram procedure the room was filled with them. Having taken physiology and anatomy classes in college, I knew approximately where the various organs were located in the human body. When the technician spent an unusual amount of time scanning areas well away and to either side of the gallbladder, unpleasant thoughts began to run through my head.

What, you might ask, can this possibly have to do with, "The best time of my life?" Well, let's see—possibly because the best time of my life might still happen. Those growths were slowly absorbing both my kidneys. At the time there were no symptoms. How long they had been growing the doctors couldn't say. Their "previous experience" with this form of slow-growing kidney cancer suggested that they might date back in time to when I began to suffer from high blood pressure about ten years earlier. There was no pain, no indication of the damage being done inside my body during all those years. Always having been a "glass half-full" person, I was now faced by a possible future with no glass at all.

As clearly as I remember my own first thoughts, I also remember my husband's first words: "Linda, you aren't alone; we'll get through this together." The most important word in that sentence was "together." I look back on that period as one frozen moment that lasted four months. Words deserted me. I simply could not find the beginning or the end of words big enough to describe what was happening.

I have always been self-reliant, stubbornly so—just ask my husband. But now I had to accept that other people were making my life's decisions and I resented it. Two surgeries were scheduled, separated by only a few weeks, with the possibility of dialysis to follow. It was an emotional rollercoaster of fears and tears that at times left me exhausted.

When my energy levels were at their lowest, I would turn always to Steve, my husband. I have told him that it was his strength that kept me going but I can never say it too many times. On more than one occasion my sobs woke him in the middle of the night and he would hold me while I cried out my despair. For that and a boatload of other reasons he will always be my *hero*. I know that he shed his own tears while I went through those surgeries but never where I would see. I know because my sister blabbed.

I'm happy to say both of the tumors were benign. I am no longer on blood pressure medication and Steve and I are walking together almost every day. Nearly a year later I am down to three-fourths of a healthy, fully functioning kidney. And I hope an infinite number of *best times of my life* are still to come with Steve.

Oh yes, they got that miserable gallbladder, too.

Jean Moelter

MATT AND JEAN DO LAUGHTER YOGA

The summer of 2010 was terrible. On July 3 my beloved mother died. Then three weeks later, completely out of the blue, my husband had a massive heart attack. Ambulance, ICU, the whole nightmare.

A few weeks into his recovery, I received an email about an event at the Steynberg Gallery: a showing of the movie *Laughology*, followed by a session of laughter yoga. I thought it might be just what we needed.

We arrived a few minutes after seven on a Friday night. The movie had already started, so I was upset. I hate to be late for anything. There were about two dozen people there, and we found seats in the back next to a thirty-ish couple.

Laughology is a documentary about the history and purpose of laughter, with interviews, silly historical reenactments, and scenes of diverse people laughing. Matt started laughing right away. In fact, everyone found it funny except me. I just didn't think it was that clever. Plus the couple next to me wouldn't stop talking, which drives me crazy.

Matt was laughing really hard. I was happy for him but also worried. His face was red and he was gasping for breath. Maybe he was laughing *too* hard. Then again his cardiologist hadn't said anything about avoiding laughter, just strenuous exercise.

The movie eventually showed a few Laughter Yoga sessions and I started to panic. They involved *touching strangers*, which I seriously can't handle.

When the movie ended, our leader, Bob, instructed us to move our chairs against the walls and form a circle. Three rules. First, fake it till you make it. Meaning, start each exercise with fake laughter and it will turn into genuine laughter. Second, no jokes or verbal humor. Third, don't hurt yourself. Ten minutes of hard laughter is equivalent to thirty minutes on a rowing machine.

My face must've shown my alarm because Matt whispered, "It's okay. Don't worry." I'd have to keep a close eye on him.

I was relieved when Bob started us off with a solo exercise. Sweep your arms up and down while saying *Ha Ha Ha*. Most people's 'Ha Ha Ha's easily converted to real laughter. Mine sounded depressed.

Next Bob told us to walk around the room, point at people, and laugh at them. Everyone's face looked scary. I wanted to scream, not laugh.

Bumper Cars was our next activity. We had to drive around the room with our hands out flat, bump into someone, push off, and laugh heartily. Then repeat with another person. I pulled over near the chairs.

Then I spotted the young woman who'd talked during the movie. She had long curly hair and tight jeans. Here was my chance for revenge. I headed toward her and she smiled at me. As I drove closer I saw that she was a lot less substantial than I was: a minivan versus a Mini Cooper. I could easily knock her down and it would look like an accident.

But at the last second I changed my mind. Violence wasn't the answer. Our hands made contact, we pushed off, and she drove away.

There were several more excruciating games. I participated but never laughed. Every few minutes I checked on Matt. At one point I caught him sitting down, but he promised he was all right. And he wanted to stay, because this was *so much fun*.

At the end of class Bob asked us to lie on the floor in a circle with our heads in the middle. He instructed us to laugh for no reason while noticing sounds and vibrations. The laughter started off strong and didn't let up. Matt was laughing so hard he had to bring his knees up to slap them. I was very worried. Also angry. Why did everyone get to have fun but me?

Then I thought of something. What if I started laughing in such an outrageous manner that it *made* people laugh? I took a deep breath and let out an insane high-pitched shrieking cackle. And it worked! The room exploded with gut-busting laughter. I did it again. And again. Absolute pandemonium.

It was thrilling to have so much power, even though Matt was one of my victims. And after a few minutes of this, I succumbed. I started to truly laugh, harder than I'd laughed for many months. And I suddenly felt nothing but love for all those nutty people. Even the movie-talkers.

Nancy G. Moore

WHAT WE FORGET

He was out. He was moving so fast he had no time for doubt. The stars fused into blades of steel as he passed. In the frigid darkness, he knew only the forward thrust of his head, the curved ligaments in his back that rose up to form gigantic wings. His wings swept aside the stars in regular beats.

Shapes he could not identify shrieked past, leaving a metallic odor. He closed his eyes, so new, in order to contain his fear and excitement. With each wing-stroke, he became more aware of his separation from everything and he wanted to cling. But his wings, unfettered at last, stretched eagerly into the burning embers of the night, and he began to sing.

On a cold planet far beyond him, a group of hunters shrouded in heavy furs knelt beside a high mountain crevasse. The distant sun edged above a peak and brought into pale relief the icy abyss at their feet. The hunters listened to the sun. They watched the play of light on snow and chanted an old story to guide the young traveler home. The details of the story were not especially important. Rather, the music, the modulation of their voices in accordance with the light, was what mattered. No one could say which came first—light or song—but all understood that new life did not come until the sun was in their voices.

He opened his eyes again. His lashes were white, crusty, the night in shreds. With one last, mighty swipe at the glancing stars, his wings folded tightly in place. He began to dive. A luminous membrane, excited by the force of his flight, gathered about him and shielded him from rivers of flame that swirled and spat on every side.

At such speed, the ordinary laws governing the coherence of matter gave way. He saw nothing so tidy as a world upon which to land. Instead, vast, dark canyons opened up at odd angles to each other, one wall randomly driven through another. He hurtled violently through intersecting planes. Sharp, flinty surfaces jabbed at his shoulders and sent him spinning. He plunged through oceans, into gaping holes, falling sideways, then rising upside down. When he tried to unfurl his wings, he could no longer feel where they were.

A high-pitched cry of fear grew within his breast. It filled the space behind his eyes and rattled against the shattered walls that obstructed his flight. Then, just as the wings were torn from his back, he heard a cry that was not his own. It came from beyond the darkness like a distant echo, except that it was not, for he could hear the tremor of many voices. With all his might, he focused on this call, matched it with his own, nursed it, prodded it, until with a sudden crack, all the fissured worlds about him flipped into line as if newly magnetized.

On the cold planet, a cluster of hunters draped in furs peered into the depths of a glacier. Shards of ice glinted in the pale sun as they chanted, listening to the light. Suddenly, a great flurry of feathers blew out of the crevasse. Everyone stopped in mid-breath. The eldest reached in and silently pulled from the clouds of down a round, little body—a tiny world.

He stared up at the ring of hooded faces, their eyes like twin stars, and then beyond them at the snowy mountains and the bright circle above. The hunters brushed feathers from his face. They gathered him into their furs and warmed him with their voices. For an instant, he understood where he was. But then he began to forget, and he cried.

Sherry Eiselen

SPEAKING OF LANGUAGE

Let me speak plainly. The English language has gotten completely out of hand. A language that supposes itself to be global, that has no qualms about incorporating words from other languages, that routinely adds slangy terms and words invented by advancing technologies, should certainly be expansive enough to steer clear of ambiguity. But, of course, that is not the case. Instead it is as though a conspiracy exists to ensure one is never entirely in control, linguistically speaking.

There have been numerous examples of English definitions evolving over time. Carnival, havoc, minister, and hundreds of other words changed their meanings. In other words, they once were other words. There was a time when you'd be better off calling your mother a hussy than telling her she was nice or pretty! (I'm tempted to let you search out their checkered history for yourself, but if you'd rather not, earlier definitions of these terms are provided below.*)

Most of us are aware that new words pop up on a regular basis. Before long they creep into daily conversation. Google becomes a verb. Bailout doesn't refer to jumping out of an airplane anymore. Slang terms are notoriously short lived and often generationally defined. Don't get me started on the use of profanity. Just don't get me started.

Ideally a word should sound like what it is. Prickly is an excellent word. It has all the required sharpness to convey its meaning. There's absolutely no excuse for words that lead one astray. Take the word ominous. What is that 'm' doing there? M doesn't belong in a word meant to convey danger! M belongs in words like hum, and it is entirely appropriate in mumble. Sinister, on the other hand, sounds quite ominous because of that hiss at the beginning. A word can be ruined by inserting the wrong sound, as that wimpy 'm' in ominous.

As far as I'm concerned, a word with too many syllables is more confusing than helpful. Disingenuous is one of those words that suffers from being overlong. All those letters strung together take our brains first one way and then another, never quite sure we've got the definition correct. You know you've seen the word before. Perhaps you can work out its meaning in context, but next time you see that same word you're puzzling over it again. You might resort to a dictionary if you're a stickler about these things. That's a sure sign something is amiss. Words like disingenuous are not to be trusted.

Another entire category of problem words is specifically designed to deceive. A grievous error in a tool of communication, don't you agree? How can we put up with a word that doesn't even want to be understood? Flammable and inflammable both mean the same thing? Come on! Bi-weekly can either mean twice a week or once every two weeks? That is just silly.

Indisposed is purposely ambiguous. "She can't come to the phone; she is indisposed." On hearing that, we only know we're going to have to call back or leave a message. Beyond that we're left with half a dozen unpleasant possibilities. Surely we could all agree to dispose of indisposed.

And that puts me in mind of a word sometimes applied to a sick person: patient. One wonders what percentage of patients are patient. Definitely a confusing term that, if not designed to deceive, certainly doesn't inspire confidence. There's another term for a sick person that's not only annoying, it deserves to be banned on the grounds of being prejudicial. Far worse than falsely claiming a patient is patient is to declare an invalid is invalid.

But I promised to speak plainly. I can offer no solution to the mess we've made of the English language. There is no going back and wiping the slate clean. There can only be forging ahead in full knowledge that half of what we say isn't exactly what we mean and the other half is going to be misinterpreted.

*Original definitions:

carnival:	remove meat
havoc:	a war cry
minister:	servant
hussy:	housewife
nice:	foolish, careless or improper
pretty:	crafty, wily
silly:	rustic or plain

Sharyl Heber

STAIRCASE OF DREAMS

I ascend the Staircase of Dreams. It seems I do this every bloody night now, moving upward in the dark, my only friend a scrawny melted-down candle. The candle shows up already lit, so there must be someone up there pulling strings.

"I don't want to be here," I holler, in case that someone mistakes my silence for comfort. "I do not want to be here!" I repeat, but it never matters what I say.

The stairs are changing on me. A week ago they were so narrow I had to turn sideways to fit. Now, they're wide and spacious. Last night the railing was flat, tonight it's carved. But, I'm always wearing the same dress, a ball gown, and I can tell you right now it's not mine. No seventeen-year-old could fill that bust. I have to bunch up the skirt in my arms to keep the dress from falling off. The material is amazing, though, shimmering in the candle light. The fabric makes a racket when I climb, shushing and crackling.

The stairs have no color. The gown looks like fibrous steel. I grip my chest where my soul should be, imagining I am filled with fog. I wonder if I am still alive but, like in a scary movie, I can hear my own heartbeat echo against these concrete walls. I look down and gray is all I see. But, here's something new. I look up and for the first time, I see a faint blue glow where the top of the stairs should be. I keep climbing.

The music startles me every time. I never know when it's going to kick in. A huge orchestra plays above me, a grand theatrical masterpiece. I raise my candle, but there's only enough light to see the step ahead of me. I'm dizzy from looking so high. Thank god there's a railing or I'd be one sorry pile of crinoline at the foot of the stairs. I'm not even close to feeling safe. One step at a time, I'm pulled like a puppet up this crazy staircase into an eerie symphony and a turquoise haze.

"Maradee!" a vile voice shouts from below, interrupting the nightmare. Every morning now, I am saved from one torment and awakened to another. The vision begins to fade around me. As I turn in my colorless gown, I look down the banister to the dull pit that is my real life. I open my eyes.

An insufferable brute hovers over my bed, flicking his cigarette ashes on my face.

"Maradee!" The Beast thunders again. I pull the covers up for protection but his smoke seeps in through the wool.

"Get your bloody arse out of bed!" he barks at me in a cockney yowl.

I don't dare say out loud what I really think, so I growl at him from under my blanket. "Grrrrrrr."

"Yeah, that's right," he says, "snarl away, like the animal you are." Then he yells, "Get up and pretend you're worth something, will ya?"

Uncle Nolan. That's what I'm supposed to call him. He's no real relation, though. My Aunt Tawny brought him home from the pub one night, and he's the meanest man in St. Claire Harbor. She was drunk when she found him. That was six years ago. Why he's still here is a mystery to me.

I'm not leaving the safety of my covers, so he rips the blankets from my grasp. He pulls me out like a rag doll and props me upright. I used to be afraid of him. Now, I just try to look invisible and hold my breath so I won't inhale the toxic residue he leaves in the air when he speaks.

He shakes me hard and points to the picture on my dresser, the angel that watches over me in the night. The frame is old and chipped, but my mother's face has magical, life-saving powers. He aims his yellow stained fingers at her and says, "Your mother says there'll be hell to pay if you're late for school."

My mum would be devastated if she knew about The Beast. I always try to turn her eyes so she can't see him, but now he's in plain view.

"She's very disappointed in you," he says to me and picks up my angel mum with his disgusting hands. He shakes the picture in front of my face. "She can see how bloody lazy you are."

I rip my mother's picture from his hands and purify it of any vile toxins with kisses. I rock her in my arms and whisper, "I'm okay, Mummy, honest. I'm okay."

Anna Unkovich

THE NIGHT THE WHIPPOORWILLS CAME BACK

Night after night, when the rest of the house went to sleep, I turned on the baby monitor to listen to the sounds of life from the far side of the house. Breath is life, I reminded myself.

It was August in Michigan, and typically hot and muggy. I found some relief by sleeping on the porch just outside of the room where I had slept as a child. This was the same porch where I had gotten my first spanking…and my second. There was no third. My father never used a switch or a belt to punish us. He didn't need to. For a man of his short stature, he had *jahunga* hands. His fingers were the same circumference as a quarter, and he was strong as an ox. After two spankings, I feared those hands, and him. Now, over fifty years later, I smiled at the strength of his convictions.

My first spanking at age five was for buying and using candy cigarettes as I "practiced" being an adult. I vividly remember Dad saying, "There will be no cigarettes in this house, candy or otherwise!" The message stuck. Neither I, nor any of my siblings ever smoked.

The second spanking was of a similar nature. Again, trying to be an adult, I colored my fingernails with crayon. The message with that bottom-warmer was that colored nails were for loose women, although my father never said it in those exact words. I think I was forty years old before I ever used colored nail polish, and then I always removed it before going home to visit my parents. I was suddenly overwhelmed with a new appreciation for what I had learned from my father.

I returned to the present and immersed myself in the sensual delights of a sixty-year old woman trying to sleep on the back porch. I had forgotten how rich the smells were on a hot night. Fertile soil, heavy with the aroma of cow manure. It brought back memories of planting crops, baling hay, and the sweat of hard work on a small farm.

I listened to the night sounds to take my mind off of the momentary lapses of sound, of breath coming through the monitor. I could hear the buzzing of mosquitoes beyond the screen and itched just thinking of them. I laughed at the memory of my father chasing down every mosquito in the house before bedtime. In the distance I heard the melody of frogs in the swamp behind the house and an occasional hoot of an owl providing percussion to nature's symphony. How beautifully black the nights were in the country.

Where were the whippoorwills? I wondered. I hadn't heard them in the three weeks since I had returned home. This sound of comfort from my childhood was missing. Other things of comfort were gone, too: the taste of Mom's warm chocolate chip cookies with a glass of milk; the smell of her blood-red roses—her only real gifts from Dad; her warm, loving smile; her laughter.

My exhausted body and sleepy mind wandered. I cherished the memories of my childhood spent in this place, as I listened to the dying breath from the monitor within, and the sounds of life from nature outdoors.

For twenty days now, I watched as my father lay slowly dying. Each night, I would pray for his breath to quiet, to be still, while at the same time fearing his release from this lifetime. With no food and almost no water, he clung to life with a tenacity and stubbornness that was evident in everything he had done for ninety-three years. As a child I had hated his bullheaded, mulish, cantankerous ways. Only now as he neared death, could I appreciate how he had shaped me and given me strength—and life.

My ears caught the sound first, and my mind came fully alert to comprehend the rhythmic "*Whip-poor-will! Whip-poor-will! Whip-poor-*

will!" I listened to the beauty of it, savoring the memories and peacefulness that it brought; it harmonized with Dad's breathing coming through the monitor and I finally fell asleep, untroubled at last.

I awakened at dawn's light. With no sound coming from the monitor, I knew that my father had died during the night—and that the whippoorwills had come home to comfort me.

David Georgi

POLE CATS

"Pole Cats" is a Santa Lucia Sierra Club group dedicated to demonstrating the benefits of trekking poles on easy day hikes. Trekking poles are similar to ski poles specially adapted for hiking. Recently they have gone high-tech. Shafts are made of strong, lightweight alloys or carbon fiber. Carbide tips securely grip slippery surfaces. Handles are made of strong, cushioned materials and are ergonomically offset. Adjustable straps and shock absorbers carry the body weight and eliminate harmful impact on hands, wrists and arms. Length adjustors allow quick and secure pole adjustments to meet differing terrain requirements. Four legs are better than two for hiking. But learning to walk on four legs takes time and determination.

Last year while visiting Kauai, my friend Greg and I decided to hike the Alakai Swamp, an ancient volcanic crater at an elevation of 4000 feet. The only open trail starts at the rim and descends into the crater. I warned Greg that I didn't know the trail conditions. I added that I was going to use my trekking poles and offered him my extra set.

Greg eyed me suspiciously and asked, "Don't you feel a bit foolish with those? You look like an Edmond Hillary wannabe."

"Poles give me stability and endurance. I don't know what sort of conditions to expect on this trail," I responded.

"Okay, bring them along. I may use them," Greg said.

At the trailhead, I offered to demonstrate some ways to use the poles.

"Look," Greg replied, "I'm going to carry them and I may use them, but don't pester me about technique. They're poles. What sort of training could I need?"

As we hiked, the trail became steep and muddy. "Poles are helpful on slippery downhill trails," I said. "Extend the poles to their maximum length and keep them planted in front of you."

"I'll use them at their regular length," he said. "I don't want to keep readjusting them."

I extended mine and took short steps, the poles giving me support and confidence. Greg awkwardly planted his poles and was able to save several slips.

The trails of Alakai Swamp meander through dense jungle and marshy swampland, connected by many steep and uneven stairs. It was a breeze to plant both poles on each succeeding step, even though some were eighteen inches high, and then hop down with the biceps serving as shock absorbers. I looked back and saw Greg following my technique.

Going uphill I planted both poles at the base of the step and used my triceps to push my body to the next level. It felt great to use upper and lower muscle groups to ascend the series of steps that would have exhausted unassisted leg muscles.

We came to a stream with algae-covered stepping stones. I planted both poles alongside the first stone and felt the carbide tips grab the slippery bottom. I stepped to the next stone, repositioned my poles and repeated the process across the stream. Greg made it across easily. "Okay," he said, "the poles *are* useful."

We reached our objective, an overlook above the Na Pali coast. We took in the jewel-like ocean and verdant valleys below.

On the way back, we ascended and descended the flights of stairs in reverse order with the poles assisting us. We were approaching the trailhead when Greg said, "I don't think I could have made it without these poles." Weeks later he purchased a set of his own.

Greg's response to trekking poles is common. People assume you can use them intuitively. In my experience, to use poles optimally, training develops appropriate muscle memory. Then you can realize such benefits as:

- More endurance, strength, stability and efficiency using all muscle groups;

- A full body workout and cardiac conditioning;

- Reduced injuries and impact on hips and knees;

- Increased fat burning.

To optimize the use of poles, appropriate software is needed. Mobility consultant, Jayah Faye Paley, has developed a training program that includes a number of skill sets to develop muscle memory.

I started Pole Cats to share this revolutionary technique. All Pole Cats hikes are easy, including uphill and downhill sections and brushed-over areas. I demonstrate basic techniques of using poles for uphill hiking.

The benefits of using trekking poles extend to frail or uncoordinated individuals. When former Sierra Club president, Ed Wayburn, was in his nineties, he gave up hiking. Paley showed him how to use poles and he continued outings for several years. The best part of hiking with poles is using all your muscle groups to glide through the landscape as a quadruped. Quadrupeds have more fun hiking. Join me on a hike; become an honorary Pole Cat. Bipeds are always welcome.

T.C. West

AUNT BESS'S SORTING CENTER

Talking with Aunt Bess was a real challenge, like doing an acrostic or working out how to open a child-safe aspirin bottle without breaking tooth or nail.

She'd always been a good conversationalist and her language was colorful and stimulating. But several years back a small cerebral accident had short-circuited her verbal wires. Nothing serious, because she went on thinking and acting with good sense, but her words got tangled. Sometimes it was hard to figure out what she meant.

For instance Bess would ask you to move that pesky kitchen stool before she barked her shin. Only she'd say chicken stool, and maybe chin instead of shin. You see what I mean. Cryptic. Words got exchanged in some associated way. You could almost imagine her brain as an untidy communication center in the middle, with words jumbled in bins like clothes piled up, not hanging neatly in closets or folded in drawers the way they are in most people's brains.

The verbal genie would get a call for a word, especially one that wasn't used too often, and went frantically sorting through the word bins, looking for the right word. Sometimes a word might be chosen because it was a good color, but wrong size or style, though usually close. Other times, a word was all wrong, but the sound of it was near enough.

Aunt Bess said oven for icebox. Until I finally learned to reverse her directions, we had a lot of spoiled food when it was my turn to put away after a meal. She'd tell us she had to clutch the train that afternoon and she wondered if there was time for her (meaning space) since she hadn't made a reservation.

When my aunt took care of me while my parents were away, I often had to think quickly to respond politely. She'd come in with a cheery smile in the morning and tell me it was time to go to bed, or ask me if I wanted something to read when it was dinnertime. I learned to answer yes, knowing she was asking if I'd like something to eat.

In fact, answering yes and smiling a lot were helpful in dealing with Aunt Bess. Since she was intelligent and kindly, whatever she was offering, no matter how it came out in words, was usually something I'd want in any case.

The other thing that happened with Aunt Bess is that the genie in her sorting center gave up on occasion and left you hanging in the middle of a sentence, kind of swinging there in the breeze, wondering if Aunt Bess was going to finish but not wanting to push her because then she'd surely forget what she was going to say. So, you'd wait, and sometimes, if you shifted your weight or hummed a little, it jogged her memory and she'd complete the sentence.

Other times, she'd just smile vaguely and drift away, probably satisfied her communication had been adequate, when really only half of what she wanted to express had gotten outside of that rummage shop her mind had become. Many, many times have I hung on Aunt Bess's words, only to find myself abandoned by her, still hanging from the noose of her unspun thought.

Bess and her disability taught me a lot. I became a great puzzle-solver, and a patient listener. Coping with her creative communications may have tipped me into psychology, and given me a head start in trying to be a compassionate and understanding parent, and in learning to forgive my own glitches.

I also learned that how someone says something isn't as important as what they mean; that it truly is the thought that counts and that words are often merely stumbling blocks.

So, Bess, wherever you are—and it's probably someplace where you're still saying angles when you mean angels—thanks. You helped me connect my ears to my mind, and to the place where you still live, right there, warming the cookies of my heart.

Let me leave you with the same words Aunt Bess left me the last time I rode in her car. She looked at me with a sweet maternal smile and told me to be sure and fasten my sleeping bag.

Anthony Toscano
A BRIDGE ACROSS TIME

Special relationships defy the distance that our notion of time demands. This is true of my most vivid recollections of my dad. He and I shared two separate summer days that jumped imaginary boundaries to become one whispered story.

Late August. We're walking along a highway made of four-foot-wide pipes that together wind a path through the marsh that connects the mainland with the island.

Dad leads. I follow.

I'm afraid of falling, but I'm determined not to show my fear. This improbable bridge carries fresh water from underground creeks to the ocean-bound residents of a cotton-candy dream named Atlantic City.

Dad walks with a faltered gait that I refuse to accept. I'd rather see him as he was and as I want him to remain. Curly hair. Shadowed beard. Gentle smile.

I slow my pace so we won't collide and break the silent spell.

I've come back from California for a visit. I want to tell my dad that I love him, but I can't untangle those three words. Instead, I ask him to repeat a remembered journey.

Crab traps roped together, slung across my back and hanging from my shoulders. Mosquitoes sinking their needled tongues into my sunburned neck. Air that smells like eggs gone bad.

In one hand I hold a burning cattail reed. Its smoldering tip sends a tiny, aromatic tornado tail skyward. My dad tells me that the smoke will chase the bugs away. I resist slapping at their persistent attack because slapping would say, "I don't believe you."

One long ago November morning we bought four new traps, folded them flat and stacked them in the trunk of our '49 Chevy. We set them down in our backyard, on top of several wooden ladders that lay resting on the ground, so the coming storms would rust the metal cages to match the muddy color of the bay. Dormant sweet pea vines wound and twisted like leather snakes around the ladders' rungs.

My dad claimed he knew the special spots, those faraway destinations where no weekend warriors dared to travel, hideaways where sly sea creatures sought refuge.

And so again, this second time, we arrive at the edge of a crippled dock. Wooden pilings, tarred with creosote, sunk deep into the land beneath the murky water, black mussels clinging to the posts like parasites.

Dad and I kneel down together on the splintered boards. He leads me through our preparations. I follow his directions.

Dad gives me a pen knife. I make an initial incision into one of the fish heads we'd brought as bait, then slip my fingers inside. Delicate bones prick the flesh of my hands. A man's hands transformed into those of a boy by my mind's eye. I poke twine through the fish head's eye sockets and tie it snug against the trap's floor. Beside the severed head I knot a bow of dirty red rag.

"The crabs will smell the fish and see the red after the blood washes away," says my dad. I nod.

Dad wraps his arms around my back. He leads our dance, as together we swing the trap back and forth through the air, leaving sufficient slack on the tow end to allow it to fly, splash, land and sink, four doors opened wide, to the bottom world where crabs crawl, desperate with hunger.

And next comes the heart of the game we play. The wordless waiting, until Dad will choose the magic moment and take the lead once more. He'll pull the slack slow and backward toward the bank, both feet planted firm and deep in oily mud reflecting rainbows. And at the last second he'll yank and guide the trap's return through summer air to solid ground.

I see all of this through younger eyes that I hold closed against the coming evening hour. Back then in 1959 we snagged two bushels' worth of blue-shelled beauties. Kept them bubbling with breath and clawing at the baskets' slats by covering them with moistened towels.

But today, inside this vain attempt to recreate an earlier occasion, we haven't retrieved a single trap before I hear my father sigh behind me. I turn to see him sitting on a sandy hill, tall blades of marsh grass waving with the breeze, chattering an ageless tune as they knock against each other.

A gust of wind takes his hair, now thin and gray and robbed of its former glory, away from his scalp. He raises his hand as if to defend himself against attack, then let's his arm drop and surrenders to fatigue.

"You lead the way this time," he says. "You pull them in. I'll follow you."

Judythe A. Guarnera
ACING THE FINAL

"Oh no! What a mess. I don't need this now. I'll never get this cleaned up before I leave for my final."

Life sometimes has an interesting way of punctuating one of its lessons. As a college re-entry student and the mother of four grown children, I believed that I was pretty street-smart and knew how to deal with life's lessons. One particular day, I realized I still had much to learn and lots of opportunities to do so.

I was prepping for my final in Health Psychology. The lesson I learned that day and the manner of delivery was anything but gentle.

My professor had given us a list of one hundred questions. He promised that if we knew the answers to those questions, we would have learned the important information he wanted us to take from the class, and we would "ace the final." The study group I belonged to divided the questions. Individually, we researched them and then met to go over the answers and take notes. We toiled for hours.

The next step was to study on my own. I was determined to do well in the final, but more importantly, I wanted to be able to incorporate this positive psychological information into my life.

The night before the test I stayed up late to study. The following morning, after my family had left the house, I was reviewing answers to the study questions in my head, as I straightened the house and cleaned up after breakfast.

I thought I was done until I discovered that one of the toilets was blocked. I angrily jiggled the handle and the toilet overflowed, yucky water running out the bathroom door and down the hall into the laundry room, almost escaping to the kitchen.

In a pre-final, sleep-deprived state frosted over with high-level anxiety, my reaction was not a pretty sight. (Not quite as bad as the sight of toilet overflow, I must admit.) How would I find enough time to clean up the odiferous mess before I left for school and the test? I knew I didn't dare leave it until I returned. The walls of my empty house rang with the sounds of my anger and frustration. "Why did this have to happen to me?" I wailed. "I don't need this now!"

A lesson gleaned during my test preparation hit me out of the blue. I answered my own question. "Yeah right, Judy, and when *would* you have needed this?" Not surprisingly, I couldn't think of a single time when I would have looked forward to cleaning up an overflowing toilet. I doubled over with laughter.

Boy, that Aaron Beck knew what he was talking about, I told myself. His Cognitive Therapy model of psychology stated that we *choose* our responses to *everything* that happens to us. An event is merely an event. The person perceiving the event is free to interpret and tell herself anything she wants to about it. What that person tells herself determines her response. Nothing external has the power to make us respond in a specific way.

In this case, there was simply an event (the overflowing toilet), my perception of that event (a catastrophe), which resulted in a thought (I don't need this now), and the resulting feelings (frustration, anger, and finally laughter).

The awareness that I had control over the thoughts and feelings that I had about the event of the overflowing toilet, allowed me to reframe the incident. My laughter focused on the acknowledgement that there would never be a time when I would have needed or welcomed that situation. I could just hear myself saying, *well, I think I'll save the overflowing toilet until next week after finals.*

This whole chain of thoughts and events really became relevant when I got to the essay part of the exam. I used the overflowing toilet story to answer a question that asked me to define Aaron Beck's model of Cognitive Therapy, giving a personal example that demonstrated how I could incorporate that model into my life

My answer outlined the less than elegant event of the overflowing toilet, along with my progression of thoughts and resultant feelings about it.

That answer earned a lot of laughs when the professor read my essay to the class. Besides gaining a new perspective which increased my sense of power and control over my responses to unpleasant events, I did, indeed, "ace the final."

Liu Yu with Dawn Cerf

DETERMINATION MADE MY DREAMS COME TRUE

No one growing up in China during the Cultural Revolution expected hidden dreams to come true. As an anemic, eleven-year-old girl, I lacked confidence that I could achieve the impossible--becoming a professional martial arts athlete. Even after my unexpected third place win in a provincial competition, I refused to believe I was special. When invited to join fifty amateurs from all over Jiangsu Province for a month-long winter training camp with the professional team, I decided to push myself as hard as possible, to see if my determination could make a difference.

Instead of using the professional all-sports camp, an elementary school near Shanghai, empty because of winter break, became our training facility. With no heat and inadequate indoor space, the training conditions were the poorest possible, enabling coaches to weed out children who couldn't tolerate the frigid weather conditions. Besides revealing who could handle the hardship of the training regimen, the winter camp showed professional athletes that other children were ready to step into their shoes if they didn't fulfill the coaches' expectations. Professional athletes had no job security and could be dismissed at any time at the whim of the coaching staff.

Attired in coveted workout uniforms, the professional athletes confidently led our kicking and jumping drills. To stand out and win the coaches' attention, I swung my leg with determination, slapping my foot with a loud crack. In my jumps, I leapt with the lightness of a kitten to reach new heights. When running, I sprinted with the power and sure-footed speed of a tiger, though I nearly blacked out by the end of each race. *I'm going to show them I want to be chosen.*

When the professional athletes performed butterfly twists, my eyes opened wide in amazement. I realized my twists were equally good. I gained confidence, adding it to everything I did.

At the end of each day, wearily crawling onto my bunk bed in the freezing classroom, I listened as the wind howled outside, shaking the window panes. Bundled in multiple layers of clothing, I huddled in the lumpy sleeping bag my father made from two blankets sewn together and stuffed with cotton. Before drifting off to a deep sleep, I repeated to myself, *I can be as good as they are.*

When the wake-up bell clanged in the dark stillness, I silently groaned with each movement of my aching, unresponsive body. After sliding out of bed, my sore muscles became rigid, shaking involuntarily in the below-freezing temperature. My constant, anemic dizziness prepared me to handle never feeling good, but I learned to dig deep within for the drive to push myself. I had five minutes to ready myself for a warm-up run. Thankfully, I always slept fully dressed to keep warm at night.

Strength training was held twice a day on the icy playground, which chilled my bones but helped me learn to go past my imagined limits. With my breath vaporizing before my eyes, I attempted to stand still in a low stance as instructed. I soon discovered, however, stillness was impossible. After fifteen minutes of no movement to help warm up my body, my tense muscles shook uncontrollably. If the coaches looked at my face, however, they saw my carefully sculpted expression of indifference despite my quivering jaw. I tried to act as if this torture was nothing. Thinking about the financial sacrifices my family was making on my behalf motivated me to continue.

Sometimes, my determination collapsed at mealtimes when I overheard the idle talk of the city coaches recruited to help the professional staff. On several occasions, they spoke about a girl from an opera family named Little Sparrow and her friend.

"Maybe those two will be selected," they mused.

I never heard them talk about me.

Pretty and vivacious, Little Sparrow had big eyes and a showy personality that captivated everyone. When asked to sing an operatic tune in the middle of the cafeteria, she belted out a lovely, high-pitched wail, bringing tears to everyone's eyes. I knew I couldn't compete with that. My quietness was my downfall. To counteract it, I continued to unleash my power during practices.

Each pair of pants I wore at the winter camp developed a hole on the inside of the knee corresponding to the bruises and scabs I acquired from doing the splits on concrete. Mama packed a needle and thread in my bag, and every Sunday I sewed up the hole to give my knee some cushion. By the end of the camp, my puckered pants bunched up at the right knee, hung crookedly. It didn't matter. I learned something important about myself while training. *My willpower can take me where I want to go.* And it did.

Mike Price

I CAN DO THIS

My wife announces, "It's time to go."

Darlene says, "Thanks, Dad, you're the greatest."

Angela says, "You're the best." I smile at my daughters and recall their teenage years. Never mind that. My baby girls are grown, married, and making their own babies. That makes me grandpa to the best grandkids in the world. I'm a ready-made baby-sitter while my wife and daughters drag their unfortunate husbands to a chick flick.

My wife asks, "Honey, are you sure you can handle them?"

"Of course I can," I assure her. "How hard can it be?"

Really now, this will be easy. Eight month old Mary is already asleep. The two year old twins, Eddie and Rita, play well together. And three year old Billie and I are best buds. I chuckle to think of my son-in-laws sitting through the tear jerker while I watch football. The game starts in half an hour.

My wife says. "Have fun playing with our grandkids. And don't let Eddie play in the bathroom again."

"Don't worry. I can handle it." The young ladies give me hugs, my wife gives me a kiss, and they say good-bye. The door closes.

"Waaaaaaah!" wails Eddie.

"Mom-mmy," screeches Rita. I scoop them in my arms. Together, we watch their parents drive away. They continue to scream until the car is out of sight. Miraculously, they become quiet, happy, and ready to play. Yep, I can do this.

Eddie immediately empties the toy bucket over his head, spilling his playthings throughout the living room. I vainly attempt to return some of the toys to the bucket. This is my first indication I might have been too optimistic.

I hear a whimper from down the hallway. I find Mary awake and confused. I pick her up and lull her back to sleep in no time. Yes, I can do this," I convince myself, until I smell something bad. "No way," I protest. "This Grandpa doesn't do dirty diapers." But I have no choice. After I finish the dirty deed, I remind myself, "I can still do this."

I carry the wide awake baby to the living room. I find more toys scattered over the floor and three tots on my dining room table. The flower vase is tipped over and Rita is splashing in the water.

"No, no, no," I say, as I pull each kid off the table. I decide to clean the mess later.

"Play with your toys, while Grandpa rocks Mary to sleep." I place her in her swing.

To my relief, they do play with their toys...for about two minutes. Now it's time to climb on Grandpa. Billie climbs on my shoulders and drums on my head. With great difficulty, I pry the three little monkeys off me. Now they want to be chased. So I chase Billy, Eddie, and Rita around and around the house. I eventually collapse in a tired heap on the floor, huffing and puffing.

"Grandpa's tired; no more chasing," I gasp. I tell myself, "That should get all their energy out. Then I can enjoy my game." Being a grandpa is hard work, but I can do it.

Now Eddie and Rita jump on my expensive leather sofa. Rita tumbles off and knocks over my reading lamp. She doesn't skip a beat as she bounces back on the couch.

I say, "My couch isn't a trampoline," as I remove the little brats from my fine furniture. I return the lamp to its proper place.

"I got to go potty," Billie cries. With that warning, I rush him to the bathroom just in the nick of time. I sigh with relief. I ensure the door is closed when we leave the bathroom. I learned that painful lesson the hard way. I remind myself the ladies will be home soon.

We return to a quiet living room. It's too quiet. Mary is swinging contently, but the other rascals are missing. I frantically search the house for those monsters. The other bathroom door is closed and the bedrooms are deserted. I enter the kitchen just in time to find Eddie on the counter, holding the flour container over his head.

"No!" I scream, as a white cloud envelops my grandson. What's taking those girls so long? I cry out loud. I stare at the clock in horror. The ladies have only been gone for fifteen minutes!

Terry Sanville

CATS

"We'll start her on three units of ProZinc, twice a day," the young vet told us. "Bring her back in a week and we'll do another glucose curve." The vet looked worried.

I petted our skinny little cat and she purred immediately, grateful to escape the brutes who had been jabbing needles in her veins all day. My wife and I moved to the animal clinic's front counter to pay our bill-a day's worth of blood sugar tests, a vial of insulin, syringes.

"Holy mother of…"

As I gazed at the computer-printed bill, the receptionist flashed a weak smile and said wryly, "It is what it is…"

Yikes.

Over the next few days, friends asked me about our 13-year-old feline's condition. When I complained about the costs, one mentioned the animal's age and said maybe it was time to "let her go." Euthanizing a furry friend is heartbreaking. But the notion got my mind spinning:

Is the high cost of veterinary care a good reason to end her life?

If my cat had a richer owner, would she have a greater right to live?

These questions are anything but academic to me, since our cat has the same chronic disease that I do—we're both insulin-dependent diabetics with health care costs that will continue until our last breaths. But over the following days, as our national health-care debate devolved into a swirling morass of finger-pointing, dogmatic proclamations, and stalemates, I knew that I wasn't just thinking about cats, but exploring the nasty ethical question of *financial determinism.*

Should a person's survival depend on their ability to pay for health care?

If America doesn't make health care affordable, are we sanctioning financial determinism and the deaths of poor and middle-class people?

These ethical questions seem to get buried in the rhetoric as complaints about government "death squads," budget and taxation impacts, and shifts from so-called free-market services to socialistic services intensify. In America's first major declaration, *life liberty and the pursuit of happiness* formed the cornerstone of our national character.

But isn't life the most basic, the most important? Shouldn't it at least be held on an equal footing with liberty—often cited as the moral basis for massive military spending?

Why aren't we as outraged about health care costs and the untimely deaths of our citizens as we are with the Taliban and Al Qaeda? Maybe the uninsured just die too quietly…and they never get enough press.

Yet every day some citizen must decide whether to pay for expensive care and medicine *or* purchase food and shelter. Others can't afford the medicine they need because a particular drug isn't on their insurance company's formulary. Still others have their liberty and happiness crushed as the cost of illness or major injury gobbles their savings, their homes, and their family's future.

Some must forego treatment because insurance administrators determine it is experimental or has not proven effective. I guess we already *have* death squads! And then there are those desperate souls who can't afford the ever-increasing cost of health services or insurance and end their lives rather than burden their families with debt.

Does *anybody* really believe that financial determinism should guide America's national health care policy? Apparently, some do. Which gets me back to my first question: Is the high cost of health services a good reason to kill my cat? There's that nasty indirect euthanasia issue again. Maybe our country should ratify a more self-centered and direct approach and place the old, the sick, the financially-strapped masses on artic ice flows (melting faster now due to global warming) and send them into the mist. Failure to adopt a national health care program *will do just that.*

When the number of folks on thin ice only included the poor, financial determinism could hide its ugly head in the political weeds—after all, *"the poor will always be with us."* But as the baby boomer population ages and younger households are faced with unemployment, high education and energy costs, and upside-down mortgages, the impact of unaffordable health care strikes at a much larger population segment, one that will likely grow.

So, if we believe "life" is important and that every American has the right to it, then who should pay for health care? *We all should!* To do so would be a reaffirmation of those truths we hold as self-evident. If we don't fix our health care system, then the divide between the haves and have-nots will broaden—and our moral compass will spin wildly for years to come. Even my cat deserves better than that.

Paul Alan Fahey

THE PLAY'S THE THING
(A Flash Play in Three Acts)

Characters:
DAISY, middle-aged. Dressed for the theater, floppy hat, beads and baubles.

HENRY, younger, debonair, dark suit.

Setting:
Present Day. Theatre lobby. Closed curtains. No scenery required.

Stage Directions:
Feel free to play this to the hilt.

ACT ONE: LOBBY TALK

Lights up. Henry and Daisy enter from opposite sides of the stage carrying rolled-up Playbills. Surprised, they meet in the center.

Henry: Daisy, darling, good to see you.

Daisy: And you, Henry. Wouldn't miss this night for the world.

Henry: Me neither. Another opening.

Daisy: Another show.

Henry: This play will be sensational. A smash for Reggie.

Daisy: Indeed, just proves every dog has his day. He's got more talent in his little finger than . . .

Henry: Not to rain on Reggie's parade, but there were a few turkeys in his past, weren't there?

Daisy: He's written some bombs, a few bumps in the road, but that's over and done with. *Que sera, sera.* Always darkest before the dawn, I say.

Henry: Me too. Every cloud has its silver lining.

Daisy: Exactly. Couldn't have said it better myself.

Henry: Reggie's finally got the tiger by the tail.

Daisy: Nothing can stop the old boy now. Look out world.

Henry: Move over sun, give him some sky. He outshines every star.

Daisy: Clear the decks, everything's coming up...

Henry: Reggie. You can take that to the bank. Count on it.

Daisy: Reggie's definitely in the money.

Henry: Come on m'honey. Take my arm, Daisy dear. Curtain up.

Daisy: Reggie's going out there tonight a has-been.

Henry: But he's coming back a star.

They link arms and exit stage left.

Lights fade

Brief interval then:

ACT TWO: INTERMISSION CHATTER

Lights up. Daisy and Henry holding drinks in plastic cups, center stage.

Daisy: Henry?

Henry: Yes, love?

Daisy: I don't like him much, do you?

Henry: Who, love?

Daisy: Reggie. He's never really been my cup of tea. Any port in a storm I used to say, but Reggie breaks the mold. He's really a horse of another color.

Henry: A horse's something. I've wracked my brain senseless. What is it about him that sticks in my craw?

Daisy: Got me.

Henry: Can't like everyone, I suppose. There's the buzzer, Daisy. Act two beginneth.

Daisy: What a life. I wouldn't trade it for a sack of gold.

Daisy and Henry link arms, turn and exit grandly stage right.

Lights fade

Brief interval then:

ACT THREE: EXIT BABBLE

Lights Up. Daisy and Henry center stage. Henry buttoning up his coat. Daisy fiddling with something in her purse. Both getting ready to leave theatre.

Daisy: Not bad for a has-been.

Henry: No. God bless dear old Reggie. He's back on top.

Daisy: You know, Henry, we'd have it made in the shade if Reggie would write us a play.

Henry: With natural dialogue, the way real people talk.

Daisy: Like you and me.

Henry: Right. Oh, well, it's not the end of the world, Daisy.

Daisy: No. The sun will come out tomorrow. After all—

Henry: Yes, Daisy dear?"

Daisy: Tomorrow's another day.

Henry: I'm here for you, Daisy.

Daisy: And me for you, Henry. I'll never walk alone, not with you by my side.

Henry: Together forever.

Daisy: And ever.

Henry: Hallelujah!

Daisy: Call me a cock-eyed optimist, Henry, but…

Henry: Yes, Daisy, darling?

Daisy: There really is no business like show business.

Arm in arm, Daisy and Henry exit stage right. Lights fade.

END OF PLAY

Chris Over

PLEASE FORGIVE ME, MS. ANDREWS, WHEREVER YOU ARE

Scouting may be a good preparation for life, but not necessarily for the next day. My parents supported my scouting career from an early age. After Cub Scout graduation, I entered that institution of higher scouting: the Webelos. Now the Webelos did many wonderful things, one of which was going on overnight camping trips to Broad Creek Boy Scout Camp.

At twelve-years of age, sleeping at a friend's house was not new; but sleeping in two-man pup tents, in the woods, with twenty other boys, was. As with all scouting events, there were strings attached. For instance, each scout had to make his own fire using only two matches. At this point in my life, I had barely mastered turning on a stove burner. The only permissible food on this camping trip was that which the scout could cook over his own fire: no sandwiches, cookies, Pop Tarts, or cereal allowed.

The day was wonderful. Everyone had a great time—until dinner. That's when the rain started. I know Central Coast residents are at least a little bit familiar with rain, but few events of nature are like a robust eastern thunderstorm. The rain soaked the firewood placed by each fire pit in anticipation of earning our fire-starting merit badge. The rain soaked our pillows, sleeping bags, and changes of clothes as it forced its way through the top of our pup tents. By eight o'clock, it was evident the rain was not going to stop. We called an emergency scout meeting.

We knew that scouts were trustworthy, but did not realize that trustworthiness came in so many different shades. After all, we were dealing with basic survival here. No one had ever gone without a meal, except as determined by our parents, which for some of us was more often than others.

For the sake of our very survival, we decided to concentrate on building just one fire, followed by each scout starting his individual fire from the roaring community fire. That wasn't really against the rules; at least, not as we interpreted them. Thirty minutes and forty matches later, the roaring fire remained entrenched in our minds, but not in the fire pit. With our bedding soaked and our stomachs empty, we did what any self-respecting group of boys would do to recoup the time: we stayed up all night.

When I returned home at noon on Sunday, I was more tired and hungry than at any time in my twelve years of existence. To my surprise, the family was getting dressed to go to Painter's Mill Amphitheater to see someone named Julie Andrews in some show called, *The Sound of Music*. I immediately lay down on the couch in our living room and fell asleep. After just a few minutes, Mother woke me to shower. She soon changed her mind after assessing my condition and concluding that I might fall asleep, collapse, stop up the drain, and drown. No shower.

We piled into our 1959 Plymouth Savoy and headed to the play. My older brother, Russ, sat in the back seat behind Mother. I sat behind Father who was driving, with my younger sister, Nan, in the middle. I immediately fell asleep again. Somewhere along the way, we stopped at a traffic light. My brother reached across Nan and shook me.

"Chris, we're here!" I immediately opened the door and shuffled out into traffic.

"Russ, get your brother back in this car right now!" Mother yelled. Laughing himself silly, he retrieved me and stuffed me back into the car in front of several bewildered drivers. The rest of the trip was uneventful; at least, that's what I'm told.

When we reached Painter's Mill, I was stupid. Literally.

"Russ, you get on one side of him, and Nan, you get on the other. Help Chris walk."

We were the center of attention. I remember my sister saying to onlookers as we stumbled along, "They only let him out on weekends."

We found our seats, and no surprise, I immediately fell asleep. It's funny how there's a hierarchy with survival needs. I think someone drew a triangle about that. My immediate need upon reaching home had been sleep. Now, almost halfway through the show and my sleep need somewhat met, I awoke in a dazed state acutely aware of another basic need.

"I want a Hershey bar."

"Russ, keep your brother quiet," Mother said.

"I want a Hershey bar," I repeated, louder and louder, as if the increasing volume would help one magically appear. I don't remember if I was close enough to the stage to distract Ms. Andrews, but if I was, let this piece serve as my humble apology. It was probably a great show.

Sue McGinty

THE MOST DANGEROUS TIME

Keening, high pitched, the sound grows in intensity. Someone screaming. Me. Neighbors step onto porches and gather in little knots. People will tell you everything is a blur at times like this. They're wrong.

Before me, in stark relief against a perfect sky, stand two men: an older one in black suit and cleric collar, a young one in uniform. A casualty officer, an Iraqi war angel of death.

"Mrs. Cynthia Lovell?" he asks.

"Is it Brad? Is my son *dead*?" I scream, hoping—God forgive me—for *injured*, even *missing*.

"Yes, Ma'am," the soldier says. "I have to read this, Ma'am. My partner usually does it, but he's sick today." His Adam's apple bobs up and down as he shows me a sheet of paper. He looks even younger than Brad. Someone's son, too.

"Wait!" I say, knowing I can't face this alone. "I'll get my husband." I run toward the kitchen, skid to a stop halfway. I keep forgetting, Jeff is gone, too. Brad flew back for his funeral six weeks ago. When my son and I hugged for the last time, I begged him to be careful—the last few weeks are the most dangerous time.

On rubbery legs, I return to the door. First my husband, and now Brad. Isn't this minister embarrassed for a God who would allow this?

"May we come in?" the minister asks.

"No, I'll come outside," I reply in a voice I do not know. My inner voice, the one I trust, whispers that there's been too much death inside already.

I step onto the porch. The minister grabs my arm, whispering ministerial words. I shake off his hand, although I know he means well.

The young man begins to read stiffly. "I'm sorry to inform you, on behalf of the United States Army, your…your…"

His voice breaks and he starts again. This time he gets only as far as "I'm sorry," and breaks down completely, sobbing his boy's heart out. The paper drifts away as he scrubs tears from his cheeks with his thumbs. "I'm sorry, Ma'am."

We look at each other, knowing that ten thousand "sorrys" would not be enough.

Still, neither the words, nor his inability to say them, are his fault. None of it is. I grab his hand with both of mine and hold on, wanting our touch to last forever. The hand could be Brad's, or Jeff's thirty years ago.

Finally, even this touch is not enough and I pull the shaking shoulders into a hug, soaking up a young male scent that reminds me of a freshly shampooed puppy. "It's okay," I say, needing somehow—in this moment—to comfort *him*. There will be time for my grief later.

"Everything will be okay," I repeat, knowing it's a lie, but having to say it just the same.

Neighbors encircle me; over and over I hear, "sorry" and "help." We need those words, and faith as well, in order to go on.

Carroll McKibben

WE ARE EACH OTHER'S KEEPERS

The recent appalling account of the nurse in Bakersfield who refused to aid a dying woman evoked chilling memories. While she cited 'company policy' in denying assistance, I relied on instinct in a similar life-and-death circumstance.

While Christmas shopping at the Town Center in Santa Maria, I stood at the entrance of a shoe store waiting for my wife to complete a purchase. Festivity filled the mall as throngs of busy, smiling shoppers moved about. I was listening to the gentle ringing of Salvation Army bells in the background and inhaling the subtle pine scent of a nearby Christmas tree when my serene mood was shattered by a frantic, hysterical scream.

"My baby!" a young woman shrieked. "Oh, God, my baby! Help me! Please, somebody help me!"

I whirled around and saw a baby girl, perhaps a year old, convulsively tossing about in a small stroller, her head jerking from side to side. A pink ribbon came loose from her golden hair and fell to the floor. Her complexion turned a deathly light blue.

A silent, petrified crowd quickly surrounded the screaming mother and struggling infant. I hoped a doctor or nurse would spring forward, but no one moved.

The baby, its nose clotted with dried yellow-green mucous, thrashed about. The panicked mother continued to scream. The inert crowd watched. Precious seconds ticked away.

Are we just going to stand here and watch this baby die? I asked myself.

My only medical background consisted of a first-aid merit badge earned in Boy Scouts many years before. Somehow I recalled a possible remedy for a choking victim: the insertion of a finger into the mouth.

I dropped to a catcher's crouch beside the little girl, placed my left hand behind her head, and forced my right index finger through her tightly clenched jaws. Tiny, sharp teeth bit into my finger, but I succeeded in reaching the back of her tongue and pushed it downward. Immediately, I felt a rush of air cross over my saliva-moistened finger and into her lungs.

The baby's chest heaved. Another rush of saliva-cooled air passed my finger. "Please call 9-1-1!" I hollered. "Someone call 9-1-1!"

The baby's bluish complexion gradually turned more normal, her breathing less labored. I held her mouth open with a finger until paramedics arrived some time later. It could have been five minutes, or ten, or fifteen. I had no idea. I had entered into a surreal world where clocks and time do not exist.

"I'll take over now," a rescuer said. He picked up the baby and placed an oxygen mask over her face. "Are you the father?" he asked.

"No," I replied.

A terrified young man stepped from the crowd and said, "I'm the father." That was the first indication the little girl's other parent was present.

"Let's go!" said the paramedic holding the baby. The father grabbed the stroller, the mother ran alongside her baby, and the entire crew jogged to a waiting ambulance. All that remained of the horrifying scene was a little girl's pink ribbon.

I had been squatting so long I didn't have the strength to rise to my feet. While aiding the baby I didn't notice any pain or discomfort. Now, I could hardly move. I placed a hand on the cashier's counter and pulled myself to my feet with the aid of my wife.

The crowd disappeared as quickly as it had gathered. I wobbled to a bench outside the store and sat down. I took a handkerchief and wiped the perspiration from my brow and the blood from my bitten finger.

"Are you okay?" my wife asked.

"Yeah," I responded. "Just give me a few minutes to let my heart quit thumping."

I never learned the name of the little girl who would now be a young lady. I doubt she remembers her brush with death. I do, and with the benefit of reinforcing a paraphrased biblical citation: We are each other's keepers, regardless of company policy.

Anne R. Allen

BAG LADY FEARS:
How I Faced Mine by Writing *No Place Like Home*

According to MSN financial columnist Jay McDonald, "Bag lady syndrome is a fear many women share that their financial security could disappear in a heartbeat, leaving them homeless, penniless and destitute."

Bag-lady syndrome can be paralyzing, according to Olivia Mellan, a Washington, D.C. therapist who specializes in money psychology. She says "Lily Tomlin, Gloria Steinem, Shirley MacLaine, and Katie Couric all admit to having a bag lady in their anxiety closet...It cuts across women of all social groups; it's not like wealthy women don't have it."

When you quit your day job to write full time—especially if you're single—those fears can escalate to nightmares, anxiety attacks, and debilitating self-doubt.

For me, they hit a crescendo when my first publisher went out of business and I had to go back to square one, writing query letters to agents and editors again like a newbie.

My magazine writing gigs had dried up, too. Either the journals had gone under or were no longer paying. I'd been out of the workforce for years and the world was in the middle of a recession. My savings were dwindling fast.

I started having a recurring nightmare about living in a rusted, wheel-less truck in some kind of dump full of rats. My skin was crawling with insects. Sometimes parts of my body would fall off. I'd wake up screaming.

One morning I woke from one of those horrific dreams to an interview on KCBX. They were talking to a successful Manhattan magazine editor who had lost her life savings to Bernie Madoff.

I got up and found my morning paper full of letters to the editor complaining about how homeless camps and panhandling were ruining our town's idyllic image.

I flashed on how the magazine editor I'd heard on NPR could be one of those scruffy people standing outside the SLO Mission with a cardboard sign—or one of those despised "bums" living in the filthy camps.

So could I.

An awful lot of us are only one Bernie Madoff or catastrophic disease away from those camps.

So I took a day off querying and outlined a story about a New York magazine editor who is not only conned by a Bernie Madoff type, but married to him, so she not only loses everything, but is accused of being complicit in his crimes. On the lam and destitute, she ends up living in a homeless camp in SLO.

For me, picturing somebody like Martha Stewart living in a tent, cooking over a Sterno stove, worrying about where to go for showers and basic bodily functions—not knowing which homeless people she could trust—helped me to walk myself through my fears and see that it would be possible to survive.

Thinking the "unthinkable" sometimes helps us to cope with our fears. If we can visualize ourselves in a terrifying situation that has a positive outcome, it can help us overcome the terror.

When I visualized my character, *Home Decorating Magazine* Editor, Doria Windsor, in a homeless camp, I pictured her surviving each of

my own fears: the lack of hygiene, the stink, the cold, hunger, loss of dignity, etc.

And if she could do it, so could I.

It also helped that I write romantic comedy. I had Doria—and my ever-unlucky sleuth Camilla—both find romance (and some perspective) as they face homelessness because of the Ponzi-scheming villain's crimes.

I researched by talking to the homeless people who panhandle in front of some of my favorite stores in Morro Bay. One woman was remarkably plucky and full of humor. She became the model for my character of Lucky.

I didn't make my homeless characters objects of pity, but strong-minded survivors who help solve the mystery of a homeless man's murder. In a way, they're the real heroes of my story.

Not long after I started the book, I got an offer from the editor of a small press to publish my backlist. Then another offered to look at the new stuff. Between September 2011 and December 2012, I published seven books. *No Place Like Home* is the most recent. It's the fourth in my series of Camilla Randall rom-com mysteries.

Things are looking up. I think making my characters face the "unthinkable" helped me face it myself. I hope it will help my readers, too.

Sharyl Heber

THE LADY IN GOLD

They reclined, basking in the humidity that held a perfume of jasmine suspended in the summer night air, the glow of the moon lighting the gazebo stage with theatrical finesse. Crickets and frogs sang in harmony to accompany the affair. Zinnia must have felt a vision stirring, for she scanned the children's faces for a faraway smile. She lit upon one with particular satisfaction.

"Let's ask our Curtsy to give us a present now," Zinnia said, calling the group to attention. "Curtsy, Darling, will you tell us a story?"

Little Curtsy froze. "I don't know any stories." Her tiny voice shook, barely audible, as she retreated into the nook of a hydrangea.

"Come on, Darling, don't be afraid." Zinnia rose to take her niece's hand and led her to the gazebo steps. "It's not required to know any stories really, not in the way you might think, with a beginning and an end. If you just have a glimpse of something, even a small fascination for it, at the simple mention of the thing, the rest just seems to spill out quite naturally."

Not convinced of this, Curtsy stiffened in the arms of her aunt.

Zinnia Winterberry possessed a repertoire of tactics to cultivate the fine art of fabrication and pursued another strategy. "If there were someone to tell about, someone magical, I wonder who it would be?" She twisted the fringe of the piano scarf she had draped about her and posed her nonchalant and rhetorical questions to the swans on the lake below.

"I know, I know!" The bolder of the Dempsey twins waved his arms from the cedar tree but Zinnia discouraged him firmly with a look.

"And, I wonder what would make something unusual."

"It's the birds," Curtsy whispered in her ear. And, from the moment these words were spoken, the Garden of Possibles would never be the same. For Zinnia's niece brought with her to Winterberry House a potent imagination and a rare talent for manifestation.

"She always has birds all around her," Curtsy said and as she did the surrounding trees filled with a chorus of bird calls.

"Does she?" Zinnia asked, delighted. "What sort of birds?"

"All sorts. Robins and hawks and ones with pretty feathers. They help her with her work."

"How divine." Zinnia marveled as the vibrant plumage of peacock emerged in shimmering turquoise next to the fountain. "And who is she?"

"She's a lady who lives in the forest," Curtsy said.

"All by herself?"

"Yes. Well, except for her birds. She wears a beautiful golden gown, and her hair is long and red and wavy all down her back." Curtsy seemed to forget that she didn't know any stories and volunteered this piece of information on her own.

"Oh yes, I see," Zinnia whispered as she watched the vision come into view. The golden goddess glided into the garden amongst the children, illuminating the night sky with the plumes of glitter in her wake. "She's magnificent." Zinnia clapped her hands.

Tiny birds flew above Curtsy's lady and larger ones trailed her on the path to the gazebo, lifting the train of her iridescent gown off the stones. The peafowl spread their fluorescent fans as she passed and she carried a mourning dove upon her finger.

Frenchy stood in awe. "*Incroyable!*" she whispered. "The child's a Winterberry, *certainement!*"

"She sings to her birds, to fetch them when she needs them," Curtsy added and nestled into her Aunt's embrace. They all listened as the woman in gold called to the swans on the lake below. She sang out with a light, soprano song and the fluid necks rose from their downy huddle to find her.

"What does she do, this lady of the forest?" Zinnia asked.

Curtsy again fell silent, pulling on the ends of her auburn hair.

"I suppose a woman such as she would spend her time tending the tall trees or minding the animals," Zinnia prompted.

"Oh, no," Curtsy corrected her quickly. She's far too busy for that."

Little Bertrum quickly lost patience with the serenity of this tale. "She's a bird brain!" he shouted, dangling from his branch in the cedar tree. "A crazy bird brain who lives in the woods. She has bats in her belfry and canaries in her knickers!"

Curtsy stood and cried out, "She does not. She's an angel, a guardian angel. She has beautiful wings that sparkle and she watches over all the children in the land who don't have mummies and daddies. She knows them all, and she loves them very much."

Vast wings like feathered crystal, which caught the silver of the moon and lit the gazebo with a platinum glow, unfolded from Curtsy's angel.

Anne Peterson
C'MON IN THE WATER'S FINE!

There comes a time in a woman's life when she can feel herself losing the battle with gravity.

At least, that time came in my life just about when I turned seventy. Forty years of arthritic decimation, total knee replacements, and multitudes of powerful prescription drugs had taken their toll, and as I warily scanned my mirror image, my faint heart took an unexpected bound.

"It's time to get real," I told my reflection. "You've become a fat old woman. Yes, I'm forced to use the 'F' word. Fat. You can hardly move because you don't get any exercise. You're sliding downhill fast." My jaw became firmer in its wad of wattles.

I knew what I must do. First I went to my local athletic club to inspect it and find out how much it would cost. The facilities were perfect for me. There was an eighty-three degree pool, nice and big, and only four-and-a-half feet deep. It regularly hosted aqua aerobics classes, which is exactly what I needed. A class was at work in the pool at that very moment, so I stayed poolside to watch the action.

An unbelievably energetic young woman with a traveling mic and loud lively music barked out orders to the twenty or so women in the pool.

"Jog it out! Knees up, knees up, knees up! And into jumping jacks! Now power it up! Higher! Higher! Let me see your belly buttons, ladies! You can do it!"

And they could. Those fat old ladies, just like me, were jumping and splashing and sweating and panting and *doing it*. I could see from how hard they were working that they must have pounding hearts and flowing circulation going. It was beautiful to watch.

Just before Christmas I asked my children not to send presents this year; just send money so I could join the athletic club. It was exciting to think that I could actually do something to change my steady plodding to the grave. I could fight back. I could regain a lot of my old health. I could put my stupid pride behind me, squeeze myself into a bathing suit, and bounce around the pool just like all the other fat old women. I didn't have to feel ashamed of my fat or decrepitude, because there were plenty of others like me...or even worse. And it didn't hold them back.

With Christmas came cash, so I signed up and with my bag of gear in hand, went to the locker room to change. A cheerful bunch of FOLs were unabashedly showing various degrees of nakedness. Their conversation was casual and friendly. They even included the occasional thin young chick showering after a weightlifting session upstairs. I guessed that the average age was about sixty-seven and the average weight one-sixty. I was right in my element. I felt only slight embarrassment. I was conscious, too, of the scars adorning my flesh.

I found my way to the pool where several women were already bobbing around, but since it was still early, I opted for a soak in the adjacent hot tub with its powerful Jacuzzi jets. I joined a couple of walrussy men and an extremely obese woman in the one hundred three degree water. The action of the jets felt good to my sore spots.

But then the teacher showed up with her music and mic. I gingerly entered the pool and was soon jogging and bouncing around with the ladies. They smiled at me encouragingly when they caught my eye. I must confess that at first glance, they all seemed like an indistinguishable bunch of FOLs. But after many sessions at the pool, Jacuzzi, and locker room, they began to emerge from their sameness as individuals, intelligent and funny. They were good company, a sisterhood of dedicated exercisers intent upon

maintaining and improving their health. Some said they'd been coming for seven years or more and all agreed that the consistent exercise made a huge difference in their lives.

It certainly did in mine. Within a week I could bend stiff toes and no longer lurched around like a drunken duck. My posture began to improve. My back hurt less. My muscles developed faster than I thought possible. And a bone density test showed improvement. People began to comment on how good I looked. I feel that I've cheated gravity a bit.

If I can do it, so can you. Fat Old Women, set aside your foolish pride and take the plunge. You won't regret it.

Jill Schaefer

OUR FIRST CAR

World War II was long over and it was time to enjoy life again. Financially enabled by a surprise windfall, my parents inherited enough money to rise up in the world and purchase our first car— brand new, beautiful, and black.

"It's a lovely day. We deserve a trip to the sea in the car," said my father. He eagerly studied the cloudless blue sky with a gleam in his eye as he anticipated his hand on the wheel and his foot on the pedal.

As if previously prepared for such a sudden campaign, my mother had her troop of six quickly organized and packed into the car with all the necessities for a day at the seaside: buckets and spades for the beach brigade, paste and cress sandwiches, and a Thermos of tea. We set off eagerly for the two-hour trip to the coast from our suburban London home.

In the excitement of getting on our way, no one minded when pleading car sickness, I asked to sit up front next to the driver. Ensconced like a princess on her throne, I perched high on a pillow next to my father. I contentedly watched the scenery slipping by from city to countryside, ever-changing, from chimney stacks and crowded dirty buildings to the wider open spaces of fresh air, thatched cottages, and cows. I clung to every moment of such bliss for I knew it would not last.

The intermittent silences of the baby sleeping, my mother dreaming and the boys engrossed in silent battle behind me, were interspersed with mutterings that increased in volume and tempo as the car ate up the miles.

"We're almost there, boys," said Mother wearily for the umpteenth time, desperately attempting to divert their interest to the passing panorama.

"First one to see the sea gets sixpence." My father's offer quickly got their attention. Unscrambling themselves to peer right, left and straight ahead, my brothers had little chance of winning the prize. Whereas, I, from my vantage point up front, glimpsed the ocean first as we rounded the corner of High Street which led down to the promenade.

As soon as we found a parking place close to the beach, unloaded everyone, and everything and set up camp, we began our enchanting day of sunshine and smiles. Yet, it seemed that we had no sooner been unleashed to discover a wonderful new world of sand, sea, shells, swimming, and seaweed than we heard Father announce, "Time to pack up and go. Hurry now, we have to beat the traffic."

"She's not sitting up front again," came the chorus from my brothers. "It's my turn. It's not fair." Mother, not about to be unseated again, sat up front with baby brother. Toppled off my throne, I was confined to the crush and cramp of the back where my brothers elbowed me into the left-over soggy sandwiches, damp towels, salty swimsuits and slimy seaweed. Left behind were the sand castles and sunny smiles as we joined the caterpillar of cars crawling along the dusty road.

Shut inside the oppressive shell of the car, we inched our way along the highway that glinted silvery in the setting sun. Our car moved slowly bumper to bumper, stopping and starting, overtaking with a "hurrah" only to be overtaken in turn. No use complaining about the state of my stomach and the pounding in my head. My parents were in the midst of a squabble.

"Are you sure I should have turned off back there?"

"No, you should have taken the turning before that."

"How can you expect me to turn off if you don't give me enough warning?"

Tempers became heated; dislike steamed off the grimy windows. Thirst went unquenched and tears undried as the trek home dragged on.

"I'm going to be sick," I gurgled between teeth clenched together in an effort to dam the up-surging tide. My brothers fell away from me with a roar of disgust.

"Get to the window quickly," urged my mother, handing me a towel as she held the baby and shoved another brother aside to free the window.

Oh, sweet release! I hung my head outside, eyes tightly closed as the breeze fanned my brow. The doleful journey continued amid the putrid odor of upset stomachs, unwashed sweat, unchanged baby, leaking oil, spilt gasoline and milk, Father's cigar, and Mother's dabbed-on perfume.

Hours later in the nightly gloom, our weary band made its way up the driveway, vowing never again to leave home. But we knew we would—next time the sun shone, faraway places beckoned, and Father's foot itched.

Mary Martin Benton

WINDS OF TIME

The only emotion Jed McCabe felt as he tossed the last rock on his brother's grave was anger. He looked at the blood-smeared boulder where Johnny's head struck when his horse fell, then shifted his gaze to the rolling mid-Texas plains. Bile seared his gut. He grabbed the reins of his brother's light-colored sorrel and then mounted his own horse. His sister, Kate, was out there, and he would find her.

Rays of sunlight pressed down on Jed's shoulders. A slip of a shadow skittered across the sand in front of him. He glanced into the early spring sky and saw the circling source of the shadow. He settled the brim of his hat against the wind. His heels bit sharply against the belly of the large, black stallion. The horse grunted, tossed his head, and moved forward with a strong gait. Jed never looked back, only wishing to put distance between him and the brother who would rather dance, whistle, and gamble than settle down with a good woman.

He pushed the horses hard for the rest of the day, alternating riding his own Big Blue with Little Jesse, his brother's horse. Both thoroughbreds were gifts from their mother. It was her belief that the powerful animals would help ensure her sons' safe return from the civil strife that was tearing the nation apart. They had proved their worth, but did nothing to safeguard the family at home.

Grit and sand whipped up by the wind pelted his face and hands. He pulled on worn, leather gloves and wrapped a bandanna over his face. The horses laid their ears back and turned their heads away from the flying silt.

As nightfall approached, Jed saw a scattered stand of cottonwoods several miles off the trail. He urged the horses in that direction. The cottonwoods grew at the edge of a wash where a small pool of water seeped against the far side of the otherwise dry gully. The trees sheltered enough buffalo grass to satisfy the horses and after watering them, he tethered them under the sparse foliage. After gathering an armful of dried roots and branches, Jed built a small fire in the bottom of the shallow wash and settled down to a meal of boiled coffee and jerked venison.

The fire's warmth radiated against his face and warmed the fabric of his trousers. The flames licked at the darkness, sending smoke and sparks floating upward. Jed watched as the embers disappeared into the night air. His thoughts flashed to the war and on the dangers of a fire after nightfall. He stood and quickly banked sand against the lively fire, cutting the blaze and drifting sparks. He leaned against his saddle, cradling a cup of coffee in one hand. The war was past, and this wasn't Tennessee.

He concentrated on the dying embers that were turning into blackened charcoal. The anger threatened to turn to grief as he thought of Johnny and what had brought them to this unforgiving land.

It had been warm the morning he and Johnny left with the 19th Tennessee Cavalry. The crops had been laid-by and Mother assured them that the harvesting would be taken care of with the help of their neighbor, Phillip Ramsey. Eleven-year-old Kate was crying and Johnny wanted her to laugh. He picked her up and whirled her in the air, singing and doing a two-step jig. Kate's tears soon turned into laughter and Jed remembered that even his own wife, Matilda, had wiped her tears and smiled.

Jed shook his head, trying to fling the painful memories from his mind. In the five years he and his brother were away, his family and his home were destroyed. When they returned, neighbors, once friendly, turned hardened faces to them and accused him and Johnny

of being traitors. In brittle words they told them their mother was dead and that Kate had gone with the Ramsey family to Texas.

He stood, his jaw clenched and tossed the remainder of the coffee into the fire. Kate held the answers to the questions that plagued him and he was anxious to keep riding. Sleep was never a welcome respite, only an inconvenience. But the horses needed the rest, and he wouldn't abuse them.

Anne R. Allen

A CENTRAL COAST WRITER MEETS THE GHOST OF GEORGE ELIOT

When I moved to the Central Coast to follow my dream of becoming a mystery writer, I had no idea of the realities of the publishing business. If I'd known, I might have chosen a less stressful profession—like cat-herding, tightrope walking, or maybe staging an all-Ayatollah drag revue in downtown Tehran.

As an actress with years of experience of cattle-drive auditions, green-room catfights, and vitriolic reviewers, I thought I'd built up enough soul-calluses to go the distance. But after nearly a decade of rejection, I was ready to give up.

I had three novels represented by a New York agency, but my savings had evaporated, my boyfriend had ridden his Harley into the sunset, and I was contemplating a move to one of the less fashionable neighborhoods of the rust belt.

Even acceptances turned into rejections: journals that accepted my stories always seemed to fold. When one editor sent the bad news, he mentioned he had a new job with a UK book publisher—and did I have any novels?

My luck seemed to have turned. I sent him one my agent deemed "too over the top," and within weeks, I was offered a contract by my new editor—a former BBC comedy writer. Included was an invitation to go "over the pond" to do some promotion.

I rented out my Los Osos house and flew to Lincolnshire, where my new publishers lived and worked in an early 19th century building on the banks of the Trent—the river George Eliot fictionalized as "the Floss."

George Eliot. I would be living a few hundred yards from the house where Mary Anne Evans—aka George Eliot—wrote *The Mill on the Floss.* An English major's fantasy come true.

At the age of…well, I'm not telling…I was about to have the adventure of my life.

I knew the company published erotica but was branching into mainstream. They'd published a distinguished poet, and a famous Chicago newspaper columnist was in residence, about to launch his new novel.

But when I arrived, I found the Chicagoan had mysteriously disappeared in a fit of pique, the erotica was hardcore, and the old factory was more of William Blake's Dark Satanic variety than Eliot's bucolic flour mill.

I tried to be enthusiastic when I was greeted by a group of friendly, but unwashed young men who presented me with warm beer, cold meat pies, and galleys to proof.

I held it together until I saw my new digs: a grimy futon and an old metal desk, hidden behind stacks of book pallets in an unheated warehouse, about a half a block from the nearest loo. My only modern convenience was a radio abandoned by a long-ago factory girl.

I admit to feelings of despair.

Then from the radio, Big Ben chimed six o'clock.

Six P.M., GMT.

Greenwich Mean Time. The words hit me with all the sonorous power of Big Ben itself. I had arrived at the mean, the middle, the center that still holds—no matter what rough beasts might slouch through the cultural deserts of the former empire. This was where my language, my instrument, was born.

I clutched my galleys to my heart. I might still be nobody in the land of my birth—but I'd landed on the home planet: England. And there, I was a published novelist.

Just like George Eliot.

And somewhere in that chilly room, I felt a presence. Somehow the spirit of Mary Anne Evans was there, telling me to hang on. I knew then that I was a writer, and no matter what stood in my way, I should always follow my dream.

Three years later, I returned to California, older, fatter (the English may not have the best food, but their beer is another story),

That Chicagoan's fit of pique turned out to be more than justified. The company was swamped in debt. Shortly before my second book was to launch, the managing partner withdrew his capital, sailed away, and mysteriously disappeared off his yacht—his body never found. The company sputtered and died.

But finally, in the past year, I have found two new publishers, and since September 2011, I've re-launched the two UK books, *Food of Love* and *The Best Revenge*, and published three new mysteries: *The Gatsby Game, Ghostwriters in the Sky*, and most recently, *Sherwood, Ltd*, which was inspired by my English adventures.

I can't help thinking the spirit of George Eliot has been watching over me.

Judythe A. Guarnera

THE DAY COURAGE SAT IN A BARBER'S CHAIR

"I want you to shave my head."

This request made in a local barbershop on a cool autumn Saturday might not sound noteworthy. Many men shave their heads. The person speaking that morning, though, was a middle-aged woman.

****

My husband, Steve, and I loved to navigate our small town of Grover Beach on foot. After breakfast that morning, we had decided to stop at Beach Barbers so Steve could get a haircut. The shop was crowded, but we found seats and passed the time listening to the chatter of other patrons and enjoying the "blast from the past"—wall to wall antiques—oldies but goodies, every one.

An hour had passed when a handsome couple who I guessed to be in their mid-fifties came in. She was a bit pale looking, but otherwise they appeared to be in good health. They stood inside the door, so still they might have been mannequins. Then the man reached over and patted his companion on the shoulder. She stepped over to the closest barber, who happened to be Al, the owner.

The woman cleared her throat several times before she spoke. The chatter dropped a few decibels and several customers looked up. A feeling of suspense seemed to settle over the shop. The other barbers stood still with their scissors and combs suspended a few inches from the heads of their clients. It was as though someone had pushed a pause button.

"I want you to shave my head," she said in a quavering voice. "You see, I have cancer. My doctor believes that I can be cured with chemo and radiation. When I started treatment, nothing happened, but then my hair started to fall out."

By now I was holding my breath. I looked over at Steve, whose moist eyes mirrored my own. You could have heard the flutter of a butterfly's wings.

"I've decided that I *will* get well. But I hate being sick. Every morning when I wake up and see handfuls of hair on my pillow, it reminds me that I'm sick. I thought if I got my head shaved, I could feel eccentric and bold rather than sick."

The man who had just sat down in Al's chair, popped up and stepped to the side with a gesture as graceful as a bullfighter sweeping his cape. Al lowered his chair and motioned for the woman to sit. He encased her neck with tissue wrap and then draped her with a cape.

The other two barbers finished with their clients. The customers paid, and then found a seat. It seemed that they wanted to share the moment with this courageous woman. Al began clipping. My scalp tingled as I imagined the little hair follicles hanging on to my head for dear life. I swiped at the tears I could no longer hold back.

The woman's partner stood close to the chair. His face revealed what might have been a mixture of love, as well as fear of what lay ahead. I wondered if he had tried to talk her out of her decision, perhaps suggested they make an appointment after hours so her shearing could be done in privacy. Why choose a barbershop instead of a beauty salon? Perhaps it was because a beauty shop is a place where women go with the expectation of a lovely hairdo. This woman had no such expectation.

There was no sign of a wig, scarf, or hat. I shuddered in the face of my own discomfort and fear of ridicule, at the same time that I admired and celebrated her courage and determination.

Al, who had kept her turned away from the mirror, whisked off the cape when he finished. She stood up and then, like a giant

snowball careening down a hill, gathered her courage and turned to face the mirror.

She gave a small gasp, gently patted the tops and sides of her bald head, and then turned to face the other patrons. I might have seen a tear glistening in her eye. Everyone stood and clapped.

"Now, it's my turn," her husband said, as he climbed into the chair, and whisked off his baseball cap to reveal thick, curly hair. Soon his salt and pepper hair joined hers on the floor.

"Anyone else want to join..." Al looked at the woman expectantly.

"Marjorie and Vic," she said.

"Anyone else want to join Marjorie and Vick?" he asked.

A gentleman with a narrow fringe of hair walked toward Al's chair.

"Don't have much to lose," he said. "Boy, will my wife be sorry she sent me for a trim."

Another round of applause followed as Marjorie and Vic exited the barbershop arm in arm.

Ruth Goodnow

RAPTOR SIGHTINGS

I play a game when I travel to the mountains from my home on the coast. I watch for hawks and count how many I see. This past weekend I counted forty-five red-shouldered hawks—fourteen on the way to Yosemite and thirty-one on the return trip. The time passes quickly and enjoyably for me as I scan the flat valley landscape. Endless miles of telephone poles and utility wires provide perfect perches for my favorite bird. Often I spot one from a distance, its unmistakable blocky-shaped silhouette sitting stock-still, a lone sentinel watching over the vast fields.

If I'm lucky, I may see one high up in flight, its tail-bands clearly visible from underneath. Sometimes I catch sight of a pair of mates hunting together, coursing low over the land. Less often, I get to see this mighty bird lift off, a sight that thrills me to the point of exclaiming aloud. Its neatly tucked wings open like a graceful parachute in slow motion to reveal a wingspan always larger than I expect and an array of distinct bands and markings that had been tucked away from view.

I've been interested in birds since I was a little girl growing up in New Jersey. My mother taught me to recognize the pretty birds of the eastern garden variety: chickadees and nuthatches, sparrows, wrens, mourning doves, and finches, as well as the brash blue jays, sassy mockingbirds, and colorful cardinals. I learned to identify their various trills and songs.

I didn't know anything about raptors and rarely if ever saw one until we moved to California's central coast eight years ago. Distinctly new and different bird song called out to us shortly after arriving here. A pair of binoculars and a consultation with *Sibley's Guide to Birds* informed us that American kestrels were mating at the top of the redwood tree in our backyard. And the rarer white-tailed kite had made a massive, gangly nest of sticks in the neighbor's California oak. We both felt honored that our new home played host to these raptors. And then after my first dramatic sightings of the lone charismatic red-shouldered hawk out on Los Osos Valley Road, I began looking everywhere for this particular foraging bird.

I find it hard to remember exactly why the hawk became my favorite bird. Its size and posture lend it a certain visual majesty. Its solitary nature draws me to it. And I admire how the hawk sits silently and motionless for long periods of time. I practice yoga and I am reminded of the challenge for me to be still when I meditate. Whenever I see this raptor, I am inclined to give it Zen-like attributes: the meditative hawk; the patient and wise hawk; the hawk, comfortable in its aloneness. I temporarily forget that the raptor is a predatory bird that perches and watches, motionless, in order to spot its prey and kill—until I see it surrounded by a pair of crows cawing frantically to protect their nest.

Walking my dog around the block the other day, I heard the hawk's high squealing *keeyuur, keeyuur* above me somewhere. I stopped to look around and spotted it high up in one of the neighborhood's tallest deciduous trees. The poplar's leafless branches provided the ideal spot, apparently for resting. Because as I watched, the raptor preened and fluffed and turned around on the branch, activities I rarely see from this usually still bird. I stood riveted, ignoring my dog's pleas to throw the ball again. I wanted to stay and watch this creature for as long as my neck could tolerate it. What I hoped for was the chance to see the hawk take flight. I played another game with myself. I would continue looking at the bird and count to twenty, slowly. If the hawk hadn't flown off in that time, I would continue on my walk with Rosie. Part of the fun of the game included good luck for me if I saw the take-off before I got to twenty.

At count seventeen, my patience rewarded me. In what seemed like slow motion, the raptor hefted onto its talons like a diver preparing to launch off a platform. Stooping into a noiseless fall, magnificent wings outspread and graceful, it pitched down and then up and away. I watched until it was out of sight, and in spite of myself, I called out to it, a catch in my voice. I wanted to thank it for the show.

Tom Harrington
FISHING WITH FRED

Like many new acquaintances, it was a patchwork of illusions from the start. But, I blithely accepted an invitation to deckhand on a twenty-eight foot commercial salmon trawler in Alaska with someone I had just met. The voluntary indenture was to be six weeks during June and July. Before departure, I called the skipper, and discovered the time had been shortened to three weeks. Initially disappointed with half an adventure, I should have offered to kiss his deck boots in gratitude as soon as I landed in Sitka.

The decision to work and live together in demanding conditions was based on the usual false advertising between new friends. Home in sunny Morro Bay, we drank coffee and walked dogs with aplomb, without inclination to notice dispositions that might prove relevant to tedious shoulder–to-shoulder labor in a confined space. There would be intense pressure to catch fish regardless of equipment, bad weather, or personal shortcomings. Who knew if one geezer novice and one topnotch fisherman with decades of experience could team up? I didn't know he could be maniacal in pursuit of fish, and he had no idea that my calm demeanor was simply old age and temporary depression. I went for adventure. He wanted to show me a good time and make money. Neither of us was aware of each other's cast of personality characters.

My day on the boat began with the dreaded engine noise piercing the quiet, followed by the rolling thunder of the anchor chain convulsing the deck above my forward berth like cannonballs dropping on a timpani drum. While the skipper was setting lines for the first tack, I tumbled out of a warm bed into saltwater-stiffened, cold, damp dungarees. Tongues were checked until after coffee and morning meds had kicked in. At first, I was to steer the boat, watch for threatening objects, and cook meals while he was fishing out of the stern pit. To avoid my potential boredom, he also taught me to run two trolling gurneys on the starboard side, while he ran two on the port side. Now I was fishing, doing regular duties, and whatever other unskilled tasks arose.

I learned how to use twenty fathom-long weighted lines with seventeen sets of tackle strung along their length. Each set had a six-foot leader, a mirrored flashing lure the size of a shoe sole, and another transparent leader with a hook disguised in a hootchie. Salmon think the hootchie is food. Some work better than others. The captain considered them, or anything else that could help catch fish, as minor deities and worshipped them with alacrity. When not working, they become demons of doom populating somber no fish catching moods.

Skipper had the eyesight of an eagle and a mental fishing computer. He studied currents, water characteristics, our ship's log, trolling depth, speed, and the tactics of seventy other boats in the fleet along this twenty-five mile stretch of inland waters southeast of Glacier Bay. He got us into salmon schools, held course over the school, ran the right gear, guided my experience, and stayed in contact with whomever else might have data, stories to swap, or fisherman's lamentations that needed tending. Curses and loathsome epithets, or humor and praise, fulminated like fierce fireworks or beautiful fountains from him depending on whether the stream of salmon coming over the transom was the right species, sustained, and kept the cash flow positive. Talk about fishing led to philosophizing, quietude cooled volubility, and privacy was a respectful attitude, not a place on board.

At any opportunity for a break in the sixteen-hour days, one of us would crash on the main bunk, coiled and ready to spring out of slumber like a jack in the box on steroids at the slightest clatter or flutter of the rigs signaling a bite. Rapid action in narrow quarters required balance. We danced across a slippery rolling deck to the

music of radios squawking, rigging clanging, engine thumping and the smell of burnt diesel fuel.

We set foot on dry land twice in three weeks. To the skipper, each episode was a necessary but malignant date with the devil, a plague of expenditures without income. I enjoyed the goofy feeling from legs not used to terra firma and the opportunity to shower and reorient myself to a real toilet seat. Shore forays ended with laundering, provisioning, and a cup of someone else's coffee.

Fate, will, the grace of humor, floating amidst reflections of snowy-peaks on quicksilver waters, and quiet moorings bathed in Alaskan sunsets, harmonized our differences. It helped that, unlike most demanding partnerships based on initial impressions, ours was intentionally short-lived.

Anne Schroeder

EBB TIME

Like rivulets of water cascading over worn boulders at the Angel Falls, the fine June mornings of Amos Merrick's life surge past, as silent and sure as the sockeye and bass that grace the lucent waters.

Overhead, a sheath of sunlight breaks through the tree line and pierces the river in front of him. Clad in a dilapidated fishing hat of camouflage green, with a motley assortment of hand-tied flies circling the band, he casts his ancient Mitchell rod and watches his lure flick the crystalline surface. He reels in and recasts, teasing the fly while watching for darting forms in the shadowy depths.

This is time at its finest, for Amos controls the pace at which his day passes. Slow to a standstill, like the stretch of river that he fishes, a man could wish for little more in these final months of his life. Today, Amos has but two hobbies, fishing and the business of letting go.

Before him, the river widens and deepens, spreading itself along the sides of the canyon.

At mid-thigh, the river tugs on his waders like a friend, patient but insistent. Amos twists, catches his balance on the shifting sand, and feels the water buffet him with its heavy, weighting rhythm. Beyond hypnotic, the river pulls him into a meditative peace, nurtured by the crackle of ozone in his ears.

He pauses and stretches, inhales the keen scent of the river, humid with the ferns rooted in the underpinnings of the bank. Above, damsel flies hover in the shadows.

He scans the cloudy sky through his polarized sunglasses, lowers his gaze and tries to penetrate the reflective water. In an hour a light drizzle will drop a fresh hatch of midges onto the water and the water will explode. But for now the fish are pensive. He is content to cast and recast, to hold his heavy, weighty magic stick and be one with the rhythm.

He has names for his favorites—bass with scars from snags or from human hands grown careless during catch and releases. He does the same now, careful to face the bass upstream so the gills don't take on water.

"There, little bud. Take off, now. Scat!"

Downstream, the water flows without pause, carving its own will, gliding toward its destiny. Sometimes it slows at a bend, ceasing its fury, calming to bubble and to spread itself shallow while sunbeams dance across the water's sheen. Then it builds again as it flows over deepening quarries, forming into rapids in a mad race against itself.

This is how Amos Merrick thinks about time, and about life in general. He has spent much of his life matching pace with the river, in what he calls his ebb time.

Seventy-four years have filled him with memories that he shares with those who love him enough to listen. Of late he is content to slip into the long ago, to recall the journey of his own river: the wild cascading of his army years, the quiet depth of hearth and home, the occasional snags and rapids that a man encounters.

This day he fishes his favorite spot. Downstream from a giant sycamore, he shares his thoughts with its silver-green branches, leaves fluttering in the lazy breeze. Drowsy from the rhythm, he daydreams precious reminders of days past.

A hesitant stirring in the underbrush brushes him awake. He turns toward the sound and sees a stout stick thrust forth from the bushes, grasped by a small boy of four summers. His grandson, Harry, stands before him, knobby knees barely covered by walking shorts, his grandmother's lunch basket dangling from his right hand. There is excitement in his eyes, breathlessness in his approach. Released by the household of women back at the cabin, Harry has gained freedom.

The river beckons to the boy, as well; and Amos hears his grandson's response:

"Grandpa, would you teach me to fish? Mama says you know all about the river."

As so happens with even the most predictable of rivers, Amos Merrick has found a new set of flurries in the ebb time of his life.

Nancy G. Moore
GOODBYE CHICAGO, HELLO SLO

We drove in from Bakersfield on what looked like the most direct route west—Highway 58. The Budget Rental truck heaved up and down hills in the sweltering heat, swinging its heavy load around one curve after another. Near the top of each hill, we searched the horizon for a refreshing ocean view, only to find yet another valley.

Our destination was Avila Beach, known for its flawless weather while Shell Beach and Pismo shiver in the fog. On that June day, however, it was at least 114 degrees from Utah to the Pacific Ocean. We wondered what we had gotten ourselves into.

SLO old-timers may have forgotten what this area looks like to the uninitiated. It's all so familiar. But for the newcomer, desert-like temperatures are among many unexpected features—such as how the dome-shaped hills obscure the ocean until you round the bend down by Shell Beach.

Yet these hills are enchanting in a way the ocean is not: At twilight, live oaks live up to their name, gesturing to each other with gnarled fingers and shaking long, mossy hair. Suddenly, a twig snaps as an invisible creature stops to look back. Dark birds of prey circle above the freeway. Here and there, a solitary ranch or winery has been dropped onto the side of a barren slope for no apparent reason. On the next hill, there's a large, planned community. If rice paddies replaced vineyards, it would look like Japan.

On the distant planet that is Chicago, you can ruin your day by failing to read the weather report. Will there be sleet, hail, or a rain/snow mix? Here, you check out the Quake Report instead. Evidently, local citizens want to know that the ground is shaking just a little every day so as to avoid one big shake, which would really ruin the weather.

Also, with so many gorgeous days, the pressure is off to grease up and go to the beach. Where the passage from LAX to Corona del Mar was once completed at jet speed, you now stroll languidly in the general direction of the ocean, stopping to read about the salmon problem or to admire a rock. Neighbors explain that it is possible to go eight months without a sand and saltwater fix.

Much is made of how San Luis Obispo is the "SLO town," as if residents were like California's tectonic plates, slowly wearing each other down and sliding mindlessly out of their grooves. If this is true, then no one from SLO is driving on 101. Those are all foreigners hurtling down the Cuesta Grade. They must be from San Francisco and Reno, or maybe Chicago.

But then who designed that on-ramp from California Blvd. to the southbound 101? It seems to have been engineered especially for Lamborghini drivers. If the oncoming traffic allows you to merge, you must shoot into the fast lane so as not to hit the truck huffing in from the next ramp, which is only seconds away. It must be that "SLO" is what you do after exiting 101, as sort of a defiant gesture.

Defiance can take many forms and in SLO-town, it takes the shape of friendliness. It's not that the sidewalks are filled with smiley faces, but rather that people withhold judgment quite a bit longer than is common in other places. At social gatherings, if you don't say what you mean the first time, or you leave out the "Los" in Osos," you can still go on talking as if nothing terrible has happened. If you lose your way looking for a light bulb at Home Depot, no one says, "Sorry, lady, but that's not my department." Even at the DMV, the staff will loan you a wrench for your license plate—a true test of civility not found in their Vehicle Registration Financial Responsibility Program, which must be based in another town.

So what does San Luis Obispo lack? Radio stations. The kind that you listen to in your car or in the kitchen while cooking. But this does

make it possible to hear the birds: finches, doves, sparrows, quail, juncos, towhees, and kinglets, hawks, and seabirds of such variety that naming them all must tax the memory of the most dedicated birder. When the sun comes out after a good rain, their songs are so bright and energetic that you must stop reading about the budget crisis and try to understand them instead. What an interesting surprise—to discover that a friendly town by the sea should also have attracted such a treasury of birds. It must be those enchanting hills.

Lillian Brown

THE MEMORY PURSE

"We came to find a horse print to finish the pocket purses for the girls," I reminded Mom as she mulled through bins of upholstery samples.

Mom had seen pocket purses in a shop in town. Always creative, she determined that we would make some for the dozen granddaughters and great granddaughters—whose names and images she intertwined and confused with long-gone friends, family and neighbors of her youth. Consisting of back pockets cut off old jeans, the denim is decorated with bits of lace, sequins, butterflies, appliquéd animals or flowers, with a diminutive print or satiny fabric forming the pouches and straps.

Bright bantam roosters the size of dinner plates peered from the dark background of the fabric squares Mom had plucked from the dollar bin. "That won't work for the pocket purses," I protested. "The pattern's way too big." Mom clamped the samples beneath her arm while continuing to search through the bin, her brown-patched, crooked hands worrying one piece after another, oblivious to my muttered comments.

Driving home, I imagined the squares of giant roosters, random tapestry and plush fabrics she'd selected adding to the collection of broken sea shells, baskets of fall leaves, pastel sketches of barren oaks, and twice-used tea bags that had sprouted on the counters and tables of my cramped house after her arrival.

At the cluttered kitchen table, I began to lay out a pouch from a cowgirl print to back a pocket Mom had decorated with an embroidered horse head and a Wrangler tag for one of my horse-crazed granddaughters. I folded a piece of the fabric, placed the pocket on top, and drew around the edge with chalk to mark where I should cut, as Mom had taught me.

The swatches of fabrics, ribbons and laces—the sewing machine set up on the kitchen table— conjured an image of Mom creating wedding gowns in our family room forty or more years ago. An ivory-silk organza train cascaded across the oversized dining table for days as she painstakingly appliquéd French lace cut-outs to the cloud-like swirl prior to a friend's formal wedding. A white straw hat became a feather and flower crown under her expert needle for my own garden nuptials.

As the afternoon moved into evening, Mom puzzled over the purse pieces, struggling to see how they would fit together. Uncertain with my sewing machine and apprehensive about cutting the fabric, Mom designated me as the sewer, while she trimmed and decorated.

"Now, what are we doing with these," she asked as she stood at the table absently fingering the various pockets, trim and partially-sewn purses.

"We're making pocket purses for the girls," I told her, forcing the sewing machine through layers of heavy denim and cotton, pushing to finish at least one bag.

Mom drew a piece of the rooster fabric from a jumble on the floor, folding it so the colorful fowl was centered on the side of a stiff tote bag.

"Mom, put it down," I said, instructing her to complete the front of the pocket she'd been gluing sequins on. "Let's finish these for the kids before we start working with the roosters," I admonished, looking at the clock, thinking of a meeting I had in the morning, and wondering why this had become *my* project.

Dropping the fabric back on the floor and stepping away from the table, she asked me to turn on the television, the purses suddenly

forgotten. After settling her in the living room in front of the TV with a partial glass of wine, I went back to finish the horse purse.

On her side of the table was a faded Levis pocket, decorated with a full-blossomed blush rose cut from a vintage chintz remnant. It was painstakingly embellished with quarter inch pink sequins, some of which had been cut to fit the swirl of the rose petals, tiny silver and deep green sparkles, and seed pearls the color of sunset. Tears filled my eyes as I tipped the jeweled creation back and forth, watching it come to life in the waning light.

The horse, butterfly, and flower purses would be for the children. My sisters would appreciate the rooster emblazoned tote bags we'd figure out how to make.

But the sunset rose purse would be mine—the prize, the gift, from my mother's artist hands.

Dennis Eamon Young
FOUND IN TRANSLATION

Sunset had begun to draw the curtains of night in Boca Chica in the Dominican Republic, as I left the noisy embrace of my party from America. I stumbled a few times on my way from our rented villa to the beach to take pictures. I ventured a tentative "*Hola!*" to the three boys we called, 'The Peanut Boys.' They flashed winning smiles as I continued across the sandy expanse toward the calm bay just beyond the palm trees.

The brilliance of the crimson, yellow, and blue-green sunset seemed slightly unreal in the middle of December, even here in the Dominican Republic. I shook my head and looked again. It was the same. I fumbled a bit getting my camera equipment out, but I was determined to stay in control enough to take pictures. Maybe I'd even sober up in the process.

My professional instincts took over as I immersed myself in the fiery embrace of water and sky in my viewfinder. I became oblivious to everything other than composing my photos. As I turned toward the jetty and rowboat, bathed in the subtlety of muted colors on the edge of fading light, I became aware that I was not alone. 'The Peanut Boys' had tied up their burro and come to stand by my shoulder to watch me. My companions called them by that name because they walked up and down the beach with their burro all day, selling peanuts, coconuts, and sugar cane to tourists like us.

The brilliance of the end of day was nothing new to them. They were more interested in the mechanics of how I changed wheels and gears as I took photos and pointed my light meter at the sky and ocean.

The biggest boy squatted in the sand and tentatively touched the side of my camera, speaking softly in musical Spanish. Being a typical American, all I could muster in response was, "*No hablo Espanol.*" We smiled at each other as the other boys crowded around us and leaned in. The first boy became a bit more insistent, cradling the camera and holding it to my face, even turning the focusing ring on the lens. One of the other boys poked at the light meter in my left hand, nudging it with a skinny forefinger. Then they all hunched their shoulders and spread their palms to the sky.

I was impressed by the simple elegance of their desire to communicate. Perhaps with us working together the loss of words could be overcome. I let the camera rest against my chest, as I spread my hands to encompass the colorful sky and water, cupping my hands to my eyes and then around the camera. I showed them how I could point my light meter at the sky and water, the needle pointing to different numbers each time.

They crowded around me, obviously intent on absorbing and understanding this information. I had each of them repeat my actions. Next I showed them how I used the numbers from the meter to set my shutter speed dial to control how fast the camera opened and closed. I let each one listen to it close. Finally I adjusted the lens aperture on the camera, so they could see the lens open wide or close down to a small size. Only then did I take a picture.

We sat there in the sand going over the steps again and again, until they could work through the whole procedure by themselves.

The next day, as I lay on the beach with my friends, I retold the tale of the night before and listened to their expressions of disbelief. I began to think that what I thought they had learned was wishful thinking on my part.

The three 'Peanut Boys' appeared, leading their burro along the beach, and stopped near our group. I invited them over and handed them my meter and camera, as one of my friends explained in

Spanish that we all wanted them to show us what they had learned the night before.

They picked up my equipment with care and to the amazement of all, each one proceeded to follow the steps to take a picture of us on the beach.

That is how three little 'Peanut Boys' triumphed over language to learn something of interest and to teach an American photographer what real communication is all about.

Curt Johnson

IN DEFENSE OF THE MAGNIFICENT SEAGULL

The Central Coast is the kingdom of the seagull. These magnificent flying machines are astounding in their beauty and athleticism. They are highly intelligent and ingenious. However, seagulls get a bad rap. What they really need is a good public relations firm to rehabilitate their gritty reputation.

As a teenager in Southern California, I would often lie on the beach looking to the sky. I watched the seagulls fly wide surveillance arcs and dive to the sea to gather their prey. Seagulls are always up for a good meal. I happily shared the contents of my meager food bag with them. Tossing a small piece of crust from a peanut butter and jelly sandwich would bring dozens of the beautiful white and gray birds to my side. My loyal friends would stay and keep me company. Our bond was unbreakable until they became convinced I was out of food.

The seagulls and I have many games to play. The 'stack the soda crackers' game consists of piling a roll of saltines one on top of another into a little tower. The pile of saltines should be placed approximately six inches from your outstretched toes, or the seagulls will cheat and rush in before the project is complete. When the tower is finished, I sit back and watch the herd of birds warily eyeing the crackers…and me. Eventually, after inching forward, one brave bird will inevitably take a shot at the tower. It falls, crackers scatter everywhere, and it becomes bird chaos—every bird for himself. That is a personality trait of seagulls when it comes to food.

Another fun game is to tuck a package of corn tortillas in my swim trunks and hike or wade to the shoreline's rock outcroppings. Once there, I pull myself to the highest point on the tallest rock. Placing a tortilla over my head, or on my head if I am feeling especially daring, I wait for the seagulls to begin their amazing aerial acrobatics. They circle, move in close, fly past, and finally come face to beak with me as they slam on their air brakes to take the tortilla. It's a link with another living creature that momentarily unites me with the whole of nature. We exist in one world with temporal living beings, communicating and breaking bread. In this case, it is actually breaking tortillas, although the communion is the same.

A few months ago, when I went to Pismo Beach, I decided to play a joke on the seagulls. One of the gull games I play is to use yellow corn tortillas as Frisbees. I toss them horizontally across the sky and the birds attempt to snatch them in midair. Once a seagull gets a tortilla it will run or fly, and the take-away game begins. The tortilla will keep changing hands, so to speak, until the seagulls have managed to break it in pieces so they are able to share a nice corn snack. It's sort of like an air rugby game with an edible ball.

On this occasion I brought the tortillas and a small yellow Frisbee. After tossing the tortillas for a while, I flipped the Frisbee into the middle of the seagull players. Some curious pecking went on until they realized I had tricked them. One large white and gray California Gull, on behalf of the group, gave me the dirtiest bird look I have ever seen. He then grabbed my Frisbee in his beak and headed for the shoreline with me running and screaming behind him. It was a hot day, the water felt great, and I eventually recovered my Frisbee about 100 feet off the shore next to the Pismo Pier. The seagull circled above laughing. I am pretty sure he might have also been screaming obscenities at me.

We have all heard the bad bird stories. They eat our garbage; sometimes they attempt to steal our food. Occasionally they will even decorate someone's head. There are some who characterize this bird conduct as felonious. In fact, seagulls are just helping us recycle. As for their targeted deposits on people's heads, the recipient is invariably the most pompous member of the group who probably deserved it.

It is never necessary to be alone on our beautiful beaches. Seagulls have been around for millions of years. There is little doubt they will be here long after our human folly condemns us to extinction. In the meantime, we can enjoy the wonders and beauty of the Central Coast. Our little flying brothers and sisters are one more piece in this magnificent mosaic of life.

Anne Peterson

I CALL IT POWER-LOUNGING

I no longer feel guilty about just sitting around. I do a lot of it, so I'm building my skills. Recently I've learned from reading trendy magazines that it's the proper thing to do. Only they call it "healing inactivity" or something fancy like "radical leisure."

After dealing with rheumatoid arthritis for 40 years, I'm tired. My rheumatologist assures me that exhaustion "comes with the territory," but that doesn't help much. You may have noticed that I said I'd been "dealing with" the disease. I didn't say I'd been fighting it. I guess some people feel obligated to struggle and thrash with their debilities, but that seems like a useless outlay of effort to me. Practice has made me adept at recognizing what kind of effort is useless and what kind is either necessary or productive. I don't do what I don't have to.

This leaves me with spare batches of time. That's when I sit or lie around doing nothing. It may be five minutes or it may be two hours. However much I can spare. If I'm outdoors, I watch whatever's around to watch: birds, plants, cars, people, water, a tiny flower shouldering its gallant way between slabs of concrete. There's always something. I look around for The Daily Gasp, too. Usually it comes unexpectedly, that fleeting moment of astounding beauty that forces me to gasp in awe and joy. I'm lucky enough to live in such a heart-renderingly gorgeous area that almost anything is fuel for The Daily

Gasp, so it's easy to achieve. I wonder whether that would qualify as deep breathing, which is also a good thing.

If I'm indoors, I usually spend my sitting and staring time in my sanctuary, my room, which I've organized to be both efficient and beautiful, in a zany way. The home shows call that "eclectic." I enjoy eyeballing the festoon of yellow cut-paper panels high on one wall. I saw and loved them in Mexico, so why not here? My homemade pictures surround me, and my colorful art supplies are visual spice.

The many plants in the room are good for long periods of ocular gazing. Lately I've taken to mentally rearranging the furniture. It takes up a lot of time, but not a whit of energy. I get lots of creative ideas from the home shows on TV which boast of redecorating on a budget of only $1000 (or whatever their schtick is); I can accomplish wonders without spending a cent.

In order to have spaces during the day for doing nothing, I have to schedule my time. I've made a list of chores and housework that *has* to be done in the course of a week, and I've allotted certain jobs to certain time slots. For instance, after I learned from an indoor plant specialist that plants prefer to get their drinks at the same time on the same day every week, I plugged that time into my schedule.

Other things are more flexible. If I get the floor mopped once a week, it doesn't really matter which day that is, unless it's back-to-back with the last mopping. My clothes get washed whenever I run out of underwear. And by the way, doing the wash is an excellent time to sit around staring because you can do nothing while doing something.

Food shopping is scheduled for twice a week. I figure I get some exercise out of it, too. But there's always a period of just sitting afterward. Fortunately, my lawn is so small that I've got it down to a five-minute routine every Saturday, followed by a long period of sitting and admiring the short grass

First thing on my daily schedule is a trip to the gym for aquarobics, which I have to do early so I can have plenty of time to do nothing. I do my obligatory exercise for the sake of maintaining whatever health I have, then as soon as I get home, I drink a cup of green tea and watch TV news. TV watching counts as sitting. I can't quite call it doing nothing, however, because I almost always watch mind-expanding things, or at least informative or funny.

My daily schedule has to include cooking the family dinner for four, which is sometimes more than I like to take on. But it's a necessity, so I plan ahead. If I start, say, an hour early, I can stop here and there during the preparation to sit and do nothing for five or ten minutes, which helps me get through the process. Then there are many of those wonderful meals that involve scrubbing potatoes, marinating chicken or beef, and tossing the whole works into the oven for a couple of hours while I sit around gazing.

If I called it meditating, I'd be revered and honored. But it's really just stopping, relaxing, enjoying the moment

A HOLIDAY COLLECTION

Sue McGinty

A DOG-GONE GOOD CHRISTMAS

Our dog Stroganoff—origin of name unknown—was the exact shape and color of an old mop. He always followed his nose, and three weeks before Christmas 1974, he followed that nose right out of town.

That chilly afternoon Chris, my ten-year-old, stared at a hole beneath our backyard fence.

"Probably ran away because you forgot to walk him," said Sean with the righteousness of a high school sophomore.

Chris balled his fists and moved toward his brother.

"That's *enough*, you two." I shouted, stepping between them. "Okay guys, what do we do now?" I asked, struggling to maintain my cool.

"Call Dad." Pat tugged at the hem of my jeans jacket. "Please, Mom. He'll find him."

I ran my fingers over my eight-year-old's crew cut. "Honey, you know I can't call Daddy right now."

"It's not that you can't. You *won't*. He doesn't come over because you're always so mean when he does." Sean's green eyes grew cold and defiant.

I sighed, knowing he had reason to be angry. My husband and I had separated last July. Suddenly I found myself struggling to raise these kids alone. I pulled the boys close. "I'll bet Stroganoff's waiting for us right now at the animal shelter."

He wasn't. The boys and I knocked on doors all over our neighborhood. Every evening after work I drove my battered Dodge Dart through Ontario's dark streets. We tacked up "Reward" signs on telephone poles as far east as Cucamonga. No one called.

I made up my mind the boys were going to have a great Christmas anyway. Late Christmas Eve I wrapped the few gifts I could afford and set them under the tree, the same as always.

Not quite. This year both their father and their dog were absent.

The next morning we made a fire and hot chocolate, and opened our presents. "Do you like your gifts?" I asked Pat as I fed hunks of wrapping paper to the flames.

My youngest son stared out the dining room window at the empty driveway and the abandoned doghouse near the fence.

Why did I get the idea that *things* could replace what they'd lost?

After church, with admonitions for me to stay in the living room, the boys disappeared into the kitchen. Sean issued orders like a general as they fixed my Christmas present—dinner with all the trimmings. Soon the smell of roast beef, baked potatoes, corn with butter sauce, and frozen boysenberry pie filled the house. I began to relax. It would be a good Christmas after all.

We were saying grace when Chris looked up from his plate. "That sounds like Dad's truck!" We all heard it then, the distinctive growl of the '66 Ford pickup.

Grace and dinner forgotten, the boys rushed outside. Bob sat in his truck, wearing a Secret Santa smile. The boys almost killed each other to get to the truck door. When they wrestled it open, a gray mop tumbled out. I stared, not believing my eyes. This mop wore a red Christmas bow and barked madly as he launched himself from one boy to the other.

"Stroganoff! Dad, this is the best present ever. Where'd you *find* him?" Sean's eyes shone like a five-year-old's.

"Running along Fourth Street, near my shop."

"That's miles from here," I said

"Looks kinda' seedy. Been gone long?"

"Three weeks," I said. The dog ran circles around the boys, all the while trying to chew the bow off his neck.

"Pulled the ribbon off one of the gifts in back," Bob explained.

Arms clamped across my chest, I peered into the truck bed. "I see that."

"Was gonna drop the gifts off tomorrow, but when I saw the dog, well...this seemed like the right time. Hope it's no bother."

"It's no bother," I said slowly.

Bob kept his eyes on me as he rubbed a spot off the truck fender with the cuff of his jacket. "You know, I wanted to stop by and see the boys. But it's just so tough to talk now, with the ways things are—you know—between us."

"I know." A coal-sized lump crept into my throat.

"Dad, can you stay for dinner?" Pat asked, his cheeks wet.

"I'm sure Daddy has plans," I said, fighting back my own tears.

"I can be a little late." Bob nudged the grass with his boot. "You don't have to do this all by yourself. I want to help."

"Yeah, Mom," Chris said. "Can't you two be friends?"

Bob searched my eyes. The aroma of our holiday feast filled the air. I hesitated a long moment, then met his eyes halfway. With Stroganoff leading the way, we moved inside.

Andrea Chmelik

HOME FOR THE HOLIDAYS

I drag my suitcase through customs and enter the Vienna airport lobby. It has been almost an hour since landing. I check my phone for messages again. Nothing. My head starts to throb. I slip the phone into my pocket and scan the crowd. Dad towers over the travelers in the hall, tall and robust. He has gained some weight since the last time I saw him. I walk over to him with a tired smile. He gives me a bear hug and for a fleeting moment, I am a little girl again. *That's how you know you're an adult. When hugs don't fix things anymore.*

"How was the flight?" Dad asks.

"Long," I answer.

"I'm sorry, honey," he says in a soft voice, and I know he isn't talking about the flight.

"Yeah, me too," I mutter.

"I wish it was under different circumstances," he continues, "but I'm so happy to have you home for Christmas." He gives me one more squeeze and takes my suitcase.

We walk past the shops that blast "All I Want for Christmas Is You." The headache gets worse.

Outside it's dark and crispy. The air is filled with the scent of fresh snow and the all-embracing joy of holidays. I take a deep breath. It is good to be back. The chill is not the wet and humid kind that penetrates your flesh and shatters your bones, like the one I left behind in New York. This one wraps you gently in an icy veil and exhilarates your senses.

We make it to the car. I get in and pull my phone out. Dad glances over quickly, then starts the engine.

"Do you want to call him?"

I hesitate before answering. "No, Dad. I don't know what I want."

We leave Vienna and drive through the countryside toward my hometown. I am staring out the window, looking at snow-covered hills. In silence, houses are puffing smoke through stone chimneys, their windows sparkling with flickering Christmas lights.

It's been five years since I was home for Christmas. In each of those years, December left a gaping hole in my heart. New York shimmered and glowed in the flood of ornaments, carols, flashing reindeer, electric angels, and laughing Santas. I was a stranger in that world. But now I am home. Tomorrow we will go to town. We will visit the Christmas market and walk from one vendor to another, their goods displayed in little wooden sheds, their faces bright from the cold wind, their hearts filled with warmth that can't quite reach their freezing fingers and toes. We will buy cups of mulled wine, cradle them in our hands, craving the heat, then feel the liquid burn its way down to our stomachs. We will cheer to people's good health, friends, and strangers alike.

"We're here," Dad says, and I open my eyes. I look up at the windows on the third floor. The lights are on. Dad takes my suitcase and we walk up the stairs. Mom is waiting at the door, her arms wide open. I hug her. I'm surprised I haven't started crying yet. We step inside and I sit down on a sofa. The stain from my coffee spill is still there, five years later. Some things last. I look at the shelf where my parents display my wedding photo. It is there, but facing the wall.

"What's that about?" I point to it.

"Well." Mom frowns. "I was going to throw it away, but Dad said I should leave it and let you decide. He turned it around, you know, in case the picture would disturb you." In that moment, I love them more than ever.

"You guys are so silly." I laugh. Tears finally fill my eyes. I get up, look at my phone one last time, then walk over to the shelf and pick up the picture. In two weeks I have to head back to New York to sign the divorce papers. Right now, I'm home for Christmas. I walk to the trash bin and toss the photo.

Judythe A. Guarnera

A CLOSE CALL—INVENTOR SAVES TRADITIONAL TURKEY DINNER

Wearing his chef's hat, Grandpa placed the holiday turkey on the dining room table. The golden brown skin was as rich looking as the gold coins of a king. Skillfully, he began the ritual carving.

Suddenly a whispered "no" stopped Grandpa in mid-air. Grandma, with a frightened look on her face, gasped, "How do we know the turkey is done? We could all die of salmonella poisoning."

None of those gathered at that table had ever known of anyone dying of salmonella from eating undercooked turkey, but I suspect that fear often sat unspoken at holiday tables. There had to be some way to tell when the turkey was done, without overcooking it and drying it out.

Knowing that dried out turkeys or a front page story of holiday feasters ill with salmonella would adversely threaten their livelihood, Goldie Kliewer, Principal Investigator, and the other members of the Commodity Marketers and Turkey Promotion Advisory Board were highly motivated to invent a device which would take the guess work out of cooking the turkey, making it safer and easier to prepare.

Enter stage left, the Dun-Rite Pop-up Turkey Timer, which revolutionized the art of cooking a turkey. A signaling device (plunger) popped up to signal that the turkey was done.

The early work on the timer took place on the Kliewer turkey ranch, formerly an airport. The old hanger had been converted to provide an apartment for Goldie, his wife and sons, and another apartment for his in-laws. In his office, which took up the remaining space, the prominently displayed "Idea Box" symbolized serious work going on.

Kliewer's teen-aged son, Steve, worked with his dad and is named on the patents. He explained that in the off seasons when turkeys weren't selling and money was scarce, it was necessary to be creative to meet ongoing needs; hence both father and son often visited the "Idea Box" for new money-saving ideas.

Although Goldie had filed his first patent in 1961, he would file nine more patents before the Dun-Rite Pop-up Turkey Timer became a reality in 1971.

As the timer went through its various permutations, action moved from the workshop to the Kliewer kitchen in the hanger. Many a turkey was roasted in Barbara Kliewer's oven. Her inventor husband left her to clean up his mess, but promised her that one day he would buy her a gold Cadillac.

Goldie had been working on the timer idea for almost eighteen years. Finally, the Commodity Marketers produced a working model of the Pop-Up Turkey Timer. Because the correct placement of the timer in the turkey was critical, it had to be sold to a turkey plant, where the timers would be inserted before the turkeys were sold to the public. The Norbest Turkey Plant bought the timers directly from Dun-Rite.

I have always trusted my pop-up timer, but never had a clue as to how it worked. The timer consisted of four parts: the outer case (usually white or blue); the little stick that pops up (usually red); a spring; and a blob of soft metal. The soft metal, solid at room temperature, turns to a liquid (melts) at about 185 degrees Fahrenheit. The melting frees the end of the red strip and the spring pops the red stick. *Voila!* The turkey is done.

As the Dun-Rite Corporation increased their sales, even reaching foreign markets, the manufacturing and packaging outgrew the hanger and they moved twice to larger buildings. Then they were approached by Minnesota Mining and Manufacturing Corporation

(3M), which purchased the turkey timer patent, as well as Goldie's other patents.

Today, Norbest turkeys still sport the timer, but there are a variety of inexpensive single use timers available in grocery stores around the holidays. Several billion turkeys later, turkey remains the main course for many holiday meals.

Mike Orton

MY FATHER'S LULLABY

I loved my dad. He wasn't afraid. He came to terms with himself when he was young, growing up in the tough neighborhoods of South Saint Jo. He stood up for himself, not by fighting, although he did his share, but by liking himself no matter what anyone thought. I remember wishing I could be like that.

My dad was fat, brilliant, played tenor sax, and was seldom home. He sold musical instruments by day and played "dance jobs" at night. In the forties, at fifteen, he was on the road touring with big bands—even playing with Kenton. I was proud of that. For him, music was everything, but he didn't talk about his life much.

Mom said he didn't want us to feel we had to live up to any expectations other than our own, but Dad's mom, Grandma Lil, disagreed. "Danny, you should tell the kids about all you done!" she'd holler. Then she'd tell us stories about how worried she was, knowing her son was on a bus tooling around the country: playing the jazz clubs; driving all night; playing cards; probably drinking. My favorite story was about how he and his friends were thrown out of restaurants in the South because some of the musicians were black.

I think that's where Dad learned to live, learned what was important, on the road, playing music in a volatile, changing, and sometimes ignorant America.

"He was just a kid," Grandma Lil would say. I always imagined someone looked out for him, mentored him, an older man, smart, hard, a good musician.

Dad taught me to see the world in a certain way, made sure I knew that "people were people," all with a heart and soul, not to judge anyone by their color, or profession. "Some of the wisest people you'll ever meet are pushing a broom," he once said. "Don't forget that, Mike." Then, he told me he was going to die.

We were in his car, an old Plymouth Valiant with a slant-six engine that wouldn't give up, but a body that was falling apart. It was the car of a traveling salesman who sold wholesale musical instruments to retailers all over Southern California. The doors were tied on with clothesline rope, the trunk and back seat filled with samples: harmonicas, guitars, and clarinets. The music was almost gone, just pieces of it left to haul around. In the glove compartment was an extra box of cigars and a candy bar or two.

My dad's face looked pasty, always sweaty regardless of the temperature. He looked at me, black hair greased with Brylcreem, blue eyes tired and swollen.

"If anything ever happens to me," he said, glancing at the windshield for a moment, one wrist resting over the top of the wheel. "If anything ever happens to me," he repeated, looking again even deeper into my eyes, "you'll be okay." That was all he said and I knew.

That night, Dad was gone on a "dance-job." Mom was heel stomping up and down the hall with an occasional sigh. I was in my brother's room where he was blasting "Deep Purple" from a makeshift car stereo with a few of his friends. It was a dark place, my brother's room, filled with fish tanks and black lights.

I gazed into a murky black-lighted aquarium, thought about all the people, about life. I wondered why there was so much pain. I thought about Dad growing up on the road, playing music, surrounded by both corruption and men of character. He made his choices and we would make ours.

I found it odd, though, a bunch of middle-class white kids in Orange County, struggling to reach adulthood, compared to my dad and the men on the bus. Of course they had something we didn't—music. It wasn't what they did; it was who they were. It identified them and allowed them entry into a brotherhood. Even at that moment, as exhausted as my dad must have been from working fourteen hours on the road and knowing he had to do it all over tomorrow, somewhere he was blowing his life's breath into his horn, eyes closed, swaying beneath the lights to a lullaby all his own.

He used to say, "Musicians are like everyone else, Mike, just people." That was the one thing he didn't understand. He thought because he had music, we all did; because he found his way, we all would. His music ended that night. Now, thirty-nine years later, I still miss him. Though sometimes, late at night I can hear the echo of his tenor blues and I whisper, "I'm okay, Dad. I'm okay."

Mary Redmond
THE IMPORTANCE OF BEING EARNEST-LY IRISH

There are only two kinds of people in the world, the Irish and those who wish they were.

If you count yourself among the latter you have good reason, because America is smitten with the Irish. More than 40 million Americans claim some Irish heritage—six times the current population of Ireland. Since 1776, over eight million Irish people have emigrated from the windswept island to our shores. In fact, the first person to step through the gates of Ellis Island was an Irish woman, Annie Moore. Annie was the beginning of a swelling human landscape called Irish-Americans, a group that has made an indelible mark on our society, and changed the way we work, play, live and laugh.

Academics have long credited the Irish as the saviors of western civilization. During the dark ages, scholars on this tiny moss-covered island laboriously recorded and safeguarded the written heritage of Greek and Roman classics and preserved both Jewish and Christian teachings. Through their thoughtful conservation, they bridged an enormous intellectual chasm, which paved the way for the light of learning to flicker again after the rise of Charlemagne.

If *The Book of Kells* and Oscar Wilde aren't reason enough to want to be Irish, William B. Yeats, James Joyce, F. Scott Fitzgerald, Frank McCourt, Flannery O'Connor, and others will certainly seal the deal. The Irish authors have marked their place in the world of literature.

They changed the way we think about ourselves and the way we see the world. And when we laugh at the little five-line stanza, the limerick, we play along with the ruse of its origin in return for the countless giggles this wanna-be-Irish poetry has given us.

Our world has been colored far beyond green with a pallet of well-known Irish-American painters. The likes of William Harnett of County Cork was known for depicting unusual objects n still life. His works included a golden horseshoe hanging from a nail and hunting loot tied to the back of a simple wooden door. Georgia O'Keefe, through her abstract arts, paved the path for women painters in America and brought the Southwest alive through her vivid portraits of an unforgiving landscape. These are but two of the Irish who have enriched our lives through art.

If the lonesome sound of "Danny Boy" tugs mysteriously at your heartstrings, it may simply be a bell that chimes familiar. Our blue grass roots hearken back to long-ago settlers from the far-away isle and can track the tendrils of their origins to Irish folk music. Country to classic, Bono to Balfe, Irish eyes have smiled upon our musical hearts as they beat their way through the songs we sing and the tunes we whistle.

From lawmakers to lawbreakers, Tip O'Neil to Boss Tweed, our government sports a long lineage of Irish-Americans. Some of our most influential presidents on both sides of the aisle trace their ancestry back to the emerald isle: twenty-two all told, including George Washington, Barack Obama, and many in between. Of course politics are not without corruption, and ours was tainted with Boss Tweed's Tammany Hall, when an infamous gang was credited with distorting the election of Andrew Jackson and using the Irish immigrant favor to corrupt the political engine of New York and beyond.

Today, as we enjoy our vastly agrarian county and marvel at its bounty, remember that this would not be possible without the help of tractors. We can thank the inventor of the modern tractor system still used today, Irishman Harry Ferguson (Massey Ferguson). As our farmland quakes upon the faults, we won't forget the father of seismology, Robert Mallet—Irish, too. At the end of the day, when all the work is done and the earth ceases to shake, Americans pick up Ireland's most favored export, Guinness. Possibly the best-selling alcoholic beverage of all time, it may be the reason the inventor of beer pong, Bryon Kaplan is—you guessed it—Irish. From splitting the atom to the cure for leprosy, the Irish have made contributions that touch our lives every day, and we have benefited from the countless humanitarians who hail from that steadfast island.

We are so besotted with the Irish and their traditions that we've even managed to come up with some of our own that aren't Irish in origin. "Kiss Me, I'm Irish" and a pinch penalty for not wearing green are utterly American and shout our desire to be numbered with the chosen.

So, here's to you if you count an Irishman among your friends, as you have the luck of the Irish, indeed. And here's to the Irish on their special day, and to the very large drop they make in the melting pot we call home.

Sherry Eiselen

MY BODY AND I

My body and I aren't speaking. The holidays are always a hard time for us, but it was particularly difficult this year. We were always at odds about something. Overeating is part of it, I understand that, but I have social obligations. My body doesn't seem to realize how important it was for me to show up at all those parties. And how would it look if I were the only one there not eating and drinking?

Our current clash isn't because I led her into temptation. Quite the opposite. I took her to the gym yesterday. Instead of being grateful, she called it punishment. She hates exercise. Usually, she doesn't object to a walk, but about mid-November she started complaining about being too tired. Okay, the holidays always mean extra work for her and not enough sleep. It stands to reason she was tired. But I get tired, too. I'm the one that has to make all the decisions and try to keep track of everything. Believe me, my memory isn't what it used to be. Frankly, I don't think she realizes how stressful life is on my side of things. If she didn't want to go to the gym, I said, a walk on a brisk January day would be invigorating. She said it was too cold. We really should get out more.

She thinks I don't understand her. I try. I really do. For example, early in December I picked out a new outfit for her. It was a black dress made of a soft stretchy jersey with a pretty red sequined cardigan and a nifty pair of red shoes. Well, the way she kept turning in circles looking at herself in the mirror, it was touch and go for a while whether she was going to let me buy it for her or not. Finally, she agreed. But the very first time she wore it, she kept pulling at the waist of the dress all evening. She kicked off the high heels as soon as we got in the car saying she wasn't sure she'd ever be able to walk again. See what I mean? Lately, nothing I do for her seems right.

My body has low self-esteem. That's the bottom line. She's begging me to get rid of all the mirrors in the house. The only thing she hates more than a mirror is a camera. I do what I can to convince her that she looks just fine. Nobody expects her to look like a teenager at her age. Nobody except her, that is.

I'm a realist. I can look around and see what other bodies our age look like. She's right in there with the pack. Not the worst, that's for sure. Plenty of bodies our age have genuine physical limitations. She should be ashamed of herself for complaining about some wrinkles…and brown spots…and flabby areas…and painful joints and…Anyway, she's not as bad off as some others. But, of course, that's not the way she sees it. She gives herself a pity party as soon as I resolve to start a diet or purchase a new skin product. If she was the decision maker, I don't think she'd ever have a mammogram or even a flu shot, for heaven's sake!

So we struggle along. I know she loses patience with me, too. I've done my share of changing over the years. Certainly she notices when I'm forgetful. I imagine she worries what will happen to her if I can't keep up my end of the bargain. Come to think of it, she probably blames me for some of her troubles. I have to admit I made some poor choices when we were younger.

But I suppose we'll get past this rough patch. The holidays are over now. Life is bound to be less hectic. The beginning of a new year is the time to make some changes. I'll keep a positive attitude. All I really want is for her to relax and not be so sensitive. I won't mention a diet. I'll just choose more salad and less dessert. Once she can fit in her favorite jeans, I'm pretty sure her whole outlook on life will improve. Before we know it, we'll be taking walks again.

Anne Schroeder

CHRISTINE'S MOTHER

"Christine's mother walks her to the bus stop," Katy remarked, twisting her toast into bite-size pieces then setting them back on the plate. "Christine's lucky."

Reaching to clear a handful of breakfast dishes from the table, I brushed a kiss across Katy's forehead and cheerfully agreed. "I guess Christine's mother loves her better."

Katy glanced up, surprised. "No she doesn't…" she started to protest, then grinned when she realized I was kidding her. I sent her off with a hug, cautioning her to hurry or she'd miss her early-bird bus. With a twinge of guilt, I watched my second-grader, bundled in her bright-blue goose down jacket and red stocking cap, running down the long driveway in the gray, frosty morning. But she skipped ahead to catch up with a friend and I started my daily routine.

That evening while I tucked her into bed, Katy reached to twist a strand of my hair and quietly told me, "Christine's mother took her to McDonald's for lunch and bought her a lip gloss and she came back to school just before recess ended. Can we do that tomorrow?"

I smiled and replied, "You bet…sometime. But not tomorrow. Daddy's taking the car and we sure can't walk that far. But sometime soon…Promise."

As I left the room and gently closed the door, I thought, *Christine is a most indulged little girl.* Christine, who skated backward on her own set of rink skates, who came out with the first computer game system in the neighborhood, whose mother walked her to the bus stop, and who is leading my daughter into unrealistic expectations of life.

I decided that if Katy felt so strongly about the attention Christine was getting, I would break out of my comfortable routine and do something about it. The next morning I dressed early and surprised her by suggesting that I walk her to the bus stop. We packed cinnamon toast and orange juice and had a picnic on a little knoll where we fed our crusts to a kitten that came by to investigate. We began a sometimes ritual of walking together and I came to know the froggy pond, the path, the friendly dog, and the children at the bus stop.

One day I met Christine's mother. After waving our children off through the back window of the disappearing yellow bus, we strolled the short distance home. Pausing at the end of my driveway, I asked her up for a cup of tea. To my surprise, she accepted and for the next two hours we shared confidences. She told me about her oldest son's musical ability, her hopes that one of her children would become a doctor, and how hard it was to join a busy family together for family dinner and prayer. Gradually, hesitantly, Donna told me of her leukemia and her numerous trips to the hospital for chemotherapy, her intolerance to germs, and her fears that Christine would not have the time with her that the older children had enjoyed.

After she left, I sat a long time just looking out my window. Finally I reached for the phone and deliberately dialed the number. The voice on the other end said, "Hello...Santa Rosa Elementary. Mrs. Anderson speaking."

"Yes, hello...This is Mrs. Schroeder. Could I leave a message for Katy in Room 5? I will be picking her up for lunch today...but I'll have her back by the end of lunch recess."

Seven months have passed and Donna is still bravely battling her illness. Christine and Katy are best friends, second-grade style. Every day when the sun comes up over our neighborhood, I say a prayer for the lady who helped me to see my world through new eyes. A very special lady—Christine's mother.

Donna Braun, Christine's mother, died three months after I wrote these words; before her death, I gave her a copy. At her request, the minister included it in her eulogy.

In the years that have passed, Donna's daughters have grown into lovely, gracious, spirit-filled women. She would be proud of her children. And I believe she would be grateful for the aunts, stepmothers, teachers, and neighbors—the women who took the time to help form them.

On Mother's Day, let us honor these women, birth mother, or surrogate.

Mary Redmond

A SLO SPIRIT TOUR

As the most frightening of fright-nights approaches, thoughts turn to ghouls, goblins, and ghosts in local graveyards. While the lore of lurking cemetery sprits is a worldwide phenomenon, from the footsteps of Charles Dickens in England's famous Highgate Cemetery to the crypt of the Voodoo Queen of New Orleans, the Central Coast is not without its own cast of creepy characters. And thankfully you don't have to brave airport security to visit them.

Just a few miles from downtown Paso Robles lurks The Pink Lady of the Adelaide Cemetery. Tales are told of late night gravesite visits when a mysterious vision appears among the tall grass, oaks slung with Spanish moss, and air thickened with coastal fog. The flowing image of Charlotte Sitton is said to waft among the graves of her children tragically taken at a young age by the diphtheria epidemic of 1882. Mrs. Sitton, later overwhelmed with grief and in a state of despair, ended her own life to spend eternity overseeing the graves.

When researchers and witnesses visited the cemetery in 2001, the lady of the hour did not make an appearance. However, when photo negatives were developed, a mysterious apparition appeared on the prints. More detailed information on this ghost-busting expedition is available by ghoooulging www.strangeusa.com.

Next stop on the local paranormal trail is Oddfellows Cemetery in San Luis Obispo (SLO), home to the Dorn's knocking Pyramid

Mausoleum. The story says if you dare to knock at the mausoleum door twelve times on Halloween night, you'll hear the thirteenth in return. Visitors may have the urge to turn around three times before knocking, which might render a stronger response. However, it might be more prudent to heed the warning posted at the entrance of the Masonic monstrosity and "Disturb Not the Sleep of Death."

Fred Adolphus Dorn built the Egyptian-style pyramid for his wife and son who tragically died during childbirth in 1905. Stranger still, Mr. Dorn never joined his departed family members in the pyramid tomb, which might explain the whole knocking issue.

While those of us living in SLO appreciate our more laidback lifestyle, it appears that eternity has these local celebrity spirits on a more specific time schedule. Mrs. Sitton can only be seen between ten P.M. and midnight on Fridays, and the haunted Dorn pyramid ghost is only available for knocking engagements on Halloween.

This spiritual sightseeing tour wraps up at San Miguel Mission. In 1848 when spirits were high and the gold rush was escalating to full speed, the old San Miguel Mission was the site of a brutal murder prompted by the age-old foils of greed and deception. Here the legend goes that a band of wandering thugs visited William Reed, owner of the mission at the time. The late night visitors murdered thirteen, including William Reed, his family, and guests.

The loot was thirty ounces of gold, which had been purchased that very day by Reed from the bandits at thirty dollars an ounce, which today would be valued at roughly $51,000. The thirteen who were slain were buried in a single tomb near the old church wall. Understandably disturbed by overcrowding, from time to time the ghost of William Reed, wearing his signature navy pea coat, greets guests in and around the mission buildings. Mr. Reed tends to adhere to his own schedule, and will occasionally be joined by his wife to the heightened enjoyment and entertainment of viewers.

Over the years much has been written about these spiritual sightings. However, San Luis Obispo actually has a number of other interesting cemeteries that are filled with local history and architectural interest. So, if you prefer to gather goodies this Halloween instead of stalking the haunted or unknown, plan a visit—during daylight—and take in the local lore. When your travels take you beyond the bounds of our county, be sure to stop at other historically haunted landmarks.

The folks at Weird California have traveled the highways of strange and marked the posts of paranormal to help you plot a trip to bizarre spots throughout the state. And for those that lean towards armchair ghost-hounding, visit www.weirdca.com for a spook-filled journey to local haunts and a cyber-trail to the Golden State's lesser known ghostly landmarks.

Rebecca Waddell
AN ALIEN FOR AN EVENING

Every year, popular movies inspire the late October parade of Halloween costumes. For 2011 there will no doubt be smurfs running amok alongside the traditional host of super heroes, princesses, supernatural and undead creatures. When I was a little girl back in 1982, the movie *E.T.* inspired a costume that would become a family legend.

At the request of my brother and my mom's own desire to see the lovable alien come to life, Mom began a several weeks-long sewing project. As the deadline for candy and costumes drew nearer and nearer, she enlisted the help of an entrenched veteran costume maker, my grandma. Together, they pulled out all the stops and finished just in the nick of time.

The end result was my brother dressed in a museum-quality reproduction of the famous alien. That balmy Halloween it must have been eighty degrees still at five o'clock, but my brother didn't care. He donned his professional-looking costume and sweated his way from house to house in the relentless search for candy. Though he nearly got heat stroke through the layers of fabric and padding, he was the most convincing E.T. on the block. And after serving to disguise my brother on All Hallows Eve, the costume was stuffed and stood in a place of honor in our living room.

The following year, we took out the stuffing and E.T. again ventured out of our home on October 31st. I finally got my turn the third year when my brother was too tall to wear it. Though the costume was stuffy, hot, and, hard to move in, I will never forget those few precious hours when I was E.T.

Diane Smith

BINGO AT BELLY ACRES

"Please, Dad, pleeease?"

"I said no."

"But why? Why can't we just open *one* present?"

"I told you. It's not Christmas yet. Now stop asking."

"Aw, c'mon, Dad! Just one!"

I detected a hint of caving in my brother's voice.

"Ask your grandmother," he said, passing the buck again. And off ran my niece and nephew to pester the living heck out of Grandma.

Long before "dysfunctional" became a household word, my family members spent as little time together as possible, with the exception of the big holidays. Then it was strictly for the turkey on Thanksgiving and out of habit at Christmas time.

It went like this. On Christmas Eve we all converged at my folks' place, the house we grew up in and that my mom lovingly called "Belly Acres," since the general atmosphere was one of incessant arguing. As adults we went to our separate corners. The yuletide found Mom in the kitchen, Dad in the garage, and me in the family room decorating the tree. When my brother Curtis and family showed up, the kids usually found me, while Curtis and his guitar disappeared.

My niece, Michele, and nephew, Jay, were eight and six the year a new tradition was accidentally born. Their whining had reached a fever pitch and Curtis, a single parent, was clearly unable to cope. When he sent them to Grandma, she must've given them the old "maybe later, we'll see" routine that she had used so many times when we were kids. Anyway, they ended up back in the family room with me. In those days I still had the energy required to reason with children.

"If you open your gifts now, you'll ruin it for Christmas day."

"We don't care!"

"You say that now, but later you'll regret it."

"No we won't!"

"Okay, say we decide to open gifts on Christmas Eve. Then next year, you won't want to wait till then and you'll be begging to open them the night *before* Christmas Eve! See how this could get out of hand?" They couldn't, so I continued. "Next thing you know, we'll be doing Christmas on Halloween!" This did little more than produce giggles.

I considered their situation. Here they were, young, excited, and having zero cousins at that time, bored to tears. Not wanting to bother Mom, I sought out my dad and asked if he had any games handy. He located a deck of cards and a box with "BINGO" and a picture of a lottery-style cage on it. I mumbled something about maybe playing poker after the kids were asleep and took the game to the family room.

There, the kids and I enjoyed a few rounds of Bingo. Pretty soon Mom joined us, then Dad. Even Curtis came and sat nearby, although he didn't join in the game. Just as I was reflecting on my brilliance in finding a clever way to distract the kids, my nephew jumped up.

"Hey, how about whoever wins the next card gets to open a present?" my nephew asked. I groaned.

"Sure, why not," my dad said, to my surprise. I didn't notice my brother leaving the room as I went about the business of distributing new Bingo cards and noisily cranking the cage.

"Bingo!" Michele announced after a while and bolted for the pile of gifts under the tree.

"Hold on." Curtis had returned, holding something behind his back. "We didn't say *which* present the winner could open, did we?" He produced something hastily wrapped in a wad of newspaper. Michele grabbed it and unwrapped a stick of gum and two used erasers. But instead of being disappointed, she began laughing.

"Just what I always wanted!" she beamed, placing the gift to her heart.

At that point we all searched the house, in junk drawers and elsewhere, wrapping found "treasures" in paper bags and old socks; the worse it looked the better. During the evening, when I thought someone was getting too many gifts, I added "instructions" inside the ones I wrapped such as, "Give to the youngest person in the room." Before long, the instructions became silly: "Put this gift back, sing the *Hallelujah Chorus*, and dance like a duck." There were even rhymed instructions, ending with *Burma Shave*.

This Christmas Eve tradition of playing games for presents continues today, although the grandkids, now numbering five, are all grown, some with kids of their own. Over the years, friends have joined us, bringing their own brand of gag gifts. And though we still refer to it as Bingo Night, we haven't played Bingo for years, preferring poker and Wii games instead. No matter. It's not the gifts or the game—it's the fun that counts. And no bellyaching!

Judith Bernstein

CHANUKAH, CELEBRATION OF LIGHT

Chanukah was a time of joy but also a time of mixed feelings for me growing up in the 50's. Joy because we had a large family Chanukah party each year, but mixed because no matter how much I liked Chanukah, I felt left out of the "mainstream." As Jews, Christmas was not for us.

In spite of jokes about putting lights on a "Chanukah Bush," most Jewish families at that time did not celebrate Christmas. Instead we observed the eight nights of Chanukah that recall a miracle that occurred while Jewish tribes were fighting the Greeks and Syrians for the right to practice their religion. The eternal light in the temple burned for eight nights, although there was only enough oil for one. So it is a holiday of triumph, hope, and enlightenment.

Still, Jewish children see signs of Christmas everywhere, from store windows to the trees festooned with lights and tinsel, and sometimes long to have both holidays. My mother often told us a story that has stuck in my mind:

"One year I had a craving for the rituals of Christmas, but especially for Santa to come down the chimney and put goodies in my stocking. So I "hung one with care," as the song goes, but instead of St. Nicklaus being there I found a large lump of coal in my stocking on Christmas morning, courtesy of Grandpa Joe."

She told this story as a cautionary tale aimed at my brother, Seth, sister, Joan, and myself. Since my father had been raised in a very religious family, he never attempted anything similar as a boy. In his annual "talk" with us children, he emphasized the uniqueness of Chanukah while regretting that it occurred about the same time as Christmas.

Each year I looked forward to the annual extended family party at the home of one of our relatives. In the weeks leading up to the party, there was frenzied shopping as each family gave a small present to each niece and nephew. There were endless discussions about food—who would bring the *kugel* (a noodle dish*)*, who would bring the *latkes* (potato pancakes), and who would make the doughnuts fried in olive oil.

And then there was planning for the Chanukah *gelt* (money), that was handed out to the children in the form of literal coins like silver dollars and symbolic coins made of chocolate and wrapped in gold foil.

"Okay," my father would say to my Uncle Sydney. "I'll buy the chocolates at Barton's candy store because it's near my office, but next year, someone else should do it." The next year, however, he bought them again because no one else had an office near Barton's.

On the big day we loaded up the car with food and presents and set off in early afternoon. In those days, people dressed up for such occasions and there was much competition among the girls to have the prettiest dress. My favorite was a blue taffeta with a large ruffle running around the bottom. The boys had little interest in clothes and were put out because they had to wear ties and suits.

When we reached the relatives, the adults usually *schmoozed* and sipped cocktails while we children were placated with hot chocolate. What we really wanted to do was skip the preliminaries and get right down to business—ripping open the fancy wrappings on the huge pile of presents that sat conspicuously and temptingly in the living room.

The official kickoff was lighting the menorahs each family brought from home. The room lights were dimmed and all the candles were lit at the same time, creating a stupendous glow that reflected in the faces of the fifty or more members of the Bernstein "tribe." We chanted the Chanukah blessing over the candles in unison, a mighty choir of voices.

Then finally the Chanukah *gelt* was distributed and the presents were opened with no attempt to "save the nice paper" as the adults always suggested. Food was put on the buffet table. The latkes were greasy—considered a good thing—and slathered with applesauce or jam and the *kugel* dishes, layers of noodles stuffed with raisins and almonds, were fabulous. After feasting, the kids had plenty of time to compare their loot before leaving around eight P.M., so the younger kids could get home at what my mother called "a decent hour."

By this time, my feelings about missing out on Christmas were long gone. My father was right: We had a unique and special holiday of our own and that was more than enough.

Christine Ahern
CHRISTMAS AT CHANTILLY FARM

The general consensus, two weeks before Christmas, was that Chantilly Farm would not have a Christmas tree.

"It's a barbaric custom," said Caroline. "Killing trees just for decoration."

"It's more than decoration," put in Rosemary. "It's tradition."

"Taking a life for a decorative purpose," said Karen. "Some tradition."

This was my first Christmas away from home, away from family. This was my first Christmas at Chantilly Farm with my new housemates. Was it also going to be my first Christmas without a Christmas tree?

"We could buy a live one," I said. "The tree lot in Burlington has potted trees. Or better yet, let's go dig one up ourselves. We can always replant it after Christmas."

"I tried that." Karen took a long drink of her chamomile tea. "Twice. One year I over-watered it. I came home to a tree, fully decorated, with not one single needle. The next year I under-watered. The poor tree looked like it had been through a fire by the time I took it down." She shook her head and frowned. "I don't need any more bad tree karma. I agree with Caroline. No tree."

"But, Caroline," I pleaded, "You have a green thumb. You could keep it alive, I'm sure."

"I could never dig up a tree." Caroline's eyes welled with tears. "You can't possibly get all the roots, and the tree feels every blow to its root system. It would stand in our living room all decorated with lights and bulbs and be in agony. I couldn't sleep at night with an agonizing tree in my living room."

"We could get a plastic one," offered Rosemary.

"*Plastic?*" a chorus of three chimed.

"Well, at least a plastic tree is an emotionless tree, and can't add to anyone's tree karma," said Rosemary.

"Yeah, but…" Karen grimaced. "It would be—plastic. We'll just start a new tradition."

"What new tradition?" I pouted.

"We could decorate something else instead of a tree."

"What?"

"The schefflera!" exclaimed Caroline. She pointed to the plant that stood in the corner of the dining room. With the aid of Caroline's green thumb this plant had grown into a *virtual* tree. Caroline and Karen jumped to their feet and dragged the schefflera into the living room. They stood it between the red chair and the couch. They opened the box of decorations that Rosemary had taken down from the attic—the act that had brought on this Christmas tree discussion in the first place.

From my seat at the table, I watched my housemates drape the large flat schefflera leaves with sparkling red and gold garland. I watched while shiny red and blue bulbs were carefully hung at the base of each leaf. I gasped a very slight gasp when the twinkling lights flashed on.

But it wasn't the same. This was a houseplant; this was not a Christmas tree.

For the next two weeks I tried with all my might to drum up some Christmas spirit, but every time I looked at the pseudo-Christmas-tree-houseplant my heart sank.

Then, on Christmas Eve, Foster brought the spirit to me, in two paper bags.

As soon as I saw him at the front door I knew something was up. He smiled conspiratorially and motioned me to follow him upstairs. He had a large paper bag under his arm and a smaller one in his hand. He opened my bedroom door and scanned the room as if he were looking for spies.

"Shhh." he said. I couldn't imagine what the conspiracy could be, but I was delighted. Once we were in the room he directed me to sit on the bed. He cleared a space on the top of my apple crate dresser, taking time to fold the clothes he removed and find new places for the books and odds and ends. Then, out of the large bag he pulled a little, real, well—real dead but *real*—Christmas tree. I actually squealed then quickly covered my mouth. One by one, out of the smaller bag, Foster removed about a dozen or so odd little ornaments: plastic elves and reindeer, tin stars, and tiny knitted mittens and stockings, and a short string of lights. After winding the lights around the little tree, Foster methodically hung the ornaments while humming "Jingle Bells." He plugged in the lights and they looked like fuzzy red and green blurs through my tears.

This was, and still is, the sweetest thing anyone had ever done for me. It touched me in that place where childhood melodies and memories dwell on Christmas mornings.

Tony Piazza

MY MOST PRECIOUS GIFT

As a young lad I was too impatient to read. Today they would improperly call my restlessness Attention Deficit Disorder, but in truth I was just being a kid as were countless other children of my era.

In second grade we had a session where we would gather in circles to read aloud. When my turn came I was usually distracted by the class clown making faces, the kid picking his nose, or the cute girl with the big dimples. I also had a nervous habit of which my teacher took note. I could not sit still, and my knee would bounce up and down as if infected by St. Vitus dance. As a result, I was failing in reading. Fortunately, my teacher took enough interest that she brought it to the attention of my mother.

Now my mother was very wise, but not in schooling. She hadn't graduated from high school, but she excelled in every job she had ever held. She was the youngest of twelve children and perhaps what she learned was survival of the fittest. She possessed, as had her mother, the ability to observe and assimilate sufficient information to accomplish any given task successfully.

My grandmother could neither read nor write, but she could study a pattern and crochet a perfect replica. She never followed a recipe, but just by the taste and feel of ingredients, put a gourmet meal on the table that would put a Cordon Bleu chef to shame. My mother was also blessed with that ability and whether she was working in an office or the five and dime, her employers recognized her abilities and she was frequently promoted. Nevertheless, she felt ashamed that she had never completed school. Consequently she always impressed upon me the virtue of a diploma and a degree that would guarantee some respectable employment. Many times she would say how she wished she could have continued her schooling. Yet, she knew that helping to keep food on her family's table had taken priority. She envied the opportunities that I had.

The following summer, after hearing about my poor reading skills, she borrowed three books from my teacher. Then, after lecturing me about the value of reading and what doors it could open, she set in motion a schedule that had us reading together for at least an hour before I could go out to play. At first I wasn't too pleased at the prospect, but as the summer wore on I found myself increasingly looking forward to the sessions. We worked hard and by the end of summer she had given me the most precious gift any parent could ever give short of love—the ability to read. From that time on, I excelled in reading and was never without a book. Reading was magic and my new-found ability opened up worlds of wonders which prior to that summer I would never have dreamed of.

As the years wore on, I was able to give back to my mother for her devotion and patience. In times of crisis, I would read to her to calm her fears, and when she became sick and was dying, I helped her escape the reality of her illness by sitting at her bedside and reading words of comfort.

I know she would be proud that I have become an author, and if truth be known, I am working hard to become a success, not for myself, but for her.

I would never had sailed around the world in a balloon, or visited twenty thousand leagues under the sea, or stood upon the mountains of Mars gazing at its twin moons, or fought pirates on the Spanish Main, without Mom's gift. I had a full, rich life of adventure without leaving the comfort of my home. Along with her love, she gave me the most precious gift—the gift of reading.

Darryl Armstrong
AN UNFORGETTABLE CHRISTMAS EVE

The coffee was three days old. I had poured it into a plastic cup with a top on it and then put it into a hole I had dug in the dirt. Every morning I sipped a little and pantomimed that satisfying expression you get from the first hot cup of java in the morning. After a few gulps I reburied it in the hole and settled back on my haunches.

Dinner the night before had been beef spiced with sauce and a can of white bread. C-rations were nutritious enough but completely without taste. The bouquet was like wet cardboard and the consistency was like half-cooked oatmeal. I planned on having it again tonight so I didn't dare form a bad opinion. We had dug in three days ago, on December 21st, the shortest day of the year.

The sergeant walked by and lightly kicked my muddy boot. This was an acknowledgement of my being there, alive and at my station. He never looked any of us in the eyes. He had some idea about not wanting to hold the last memory of anybody being their eyes. I accepted the kick and leaned into the rifle tripod as if this was the only encouragement I needed to keep going.

I had been looking at this same open space for three days and could shut my eyes and recreate every feature: two scraggly trees on the left, a downward sloping area directly in front, and rock and ferns on the right. A fire fight erupted about every six hours or so.

Dino slept beside me. We traded out every four hours in the trench. He had pulled his helmet over his eyes and wadded his poncho around his ears and neck to keep the bugs out. Dino never moved when he slept. An ability he developed from earlier training as a sentry in the trees.

Finally it was my turn to rest in the mud. As I slid down the dirt wall my mind went back to Florida—home, and the house near the river that emptied into the Gulf. I grew up running barefoot through wet ground and soggy terrain so this environment—the smells of earth, the deep wet smell of rotting leaves and roots—was not so unusual. Viet Nam felt like home. I played in mud puddles as a kid and dug in the moist, rooted ground. I loved the sandy delta near the river. It held brackish water and was strewn with oyster shells, fiddler crab, horseshoe crab, and limestone rocks. Living there developed a respect for flora and fauna.

The *pop, pop* started way down the line on the left side and like a growing wave it came toward us, the sound changing to more of a *pock, pock* sound. Dino flipped his safety and squeezed off the first round while pushing me with his boot. It wasn't necessary; I was already climbing up with my piece and tripod, which I rested on the edge of the trench.

I watched for fire coming out of gun muzzles in the early morning light and then shot toward them. None of us were really all that great as marksmen, but neither was the enemy.

My eyes caught the movement about halfway between us—a mongrel dog about the size of a retriever, with a gaunt body and hanging teats indicating recently whelped puppies. She was in the middle of the crossfire and angled to one side and then the other as guns fired back and forth. Her path was crooked but her forward progress remained resolute.

As she crossed in front of us, each soldier on both sides voluntarily withheld their firing until she was clear. It was as if she deserved some special reverence. She hung her head and kept moving toward my right, finally passing directly in front of me. I, too, held my fire until she had cleared.

She was greeted at the opening of the den under the rocks and ferns by two furry pups, which seemed glad to have their mother back. She sniffed them and licked at them as she pushed them back to safety.

It was a long while until I could begin firing again, and when I did, I found myself aiming way too high to be of consequence. Such an odd way to witness the spirit of Christmas, but forty-eight years later, it still comes back to me on Christmas Eve.

David Schwab

THANKS, MOM

I can still see my mom standing in the kitchen of the house I grew up in. Her slender frame, small waist, long legs, and strawberry blonde hair showed off the Viking heritage and Scandinavian features she passed on to me. Thanks, Mom.

We had the typical 1950's tract home life of post- World War II America. I lived in the same house and went to elementary, junior, and senior high school from the same front door.

I spent my summer vacations at the lake with her father. He was the hunter and fisherman of the family. Nearby was the bowling alley where I fell in love with my first summer camping girl to the tune of "Surf City" by the Beach Boys.

I was married and both of my children were in college when we went with mom for her procedure at the hospital. The doctor said, "It's lung cancer, it's inoperable, and it's terminal." He said four to eight months. Mom admitted that she knew it was bad when we all walked into her room and she saw the expression on our faces. There she was sitting up in a hospital bed in a private room, still beautiful even in her seventies.

Mom loved to sit and talk over a cup of coffee. She taught me how our temporary personal problems are insignificant compared to the vastness of the ocean or the night sky. She complained that just when your children get interesting to talk to, they move away.

We had the gift of time, although it was a double-edged blade. We had the time to say what we needed and wanted to say, but we also were going to have to watch her slowly fade away.

I had my annual ten-day motorcycle trip planned in October. Mom said, "Go if you want to." So I loaded up my bike and kissed her good-bye. A couple of hours later I was in the high desert heading north and it hit me. *What was I doing riding out here?* The voice of a friend saying, *There will be more rides,* started playing in my mind. I pulled over, left a message, and headed home to Mom. I cried like a two-hundred-fifty pound baby dressed in black leather. It felt good to let it out. I have not cried like that again until I started this piece.

I spent the next week at Mom's. She was starting to look tired and she was losing weight.

Thanksgiving came and we all gathered around the turkey dinner. Mom said she didn't want to come into the dining room. This was going to be the first Thanksgiving without her at the table.

At Christmas my brother got a ten-foot Christmas tree. We put the 1930's train from Mom's childhood around the base. The lights went on slowly, then just a few ornaments at a time. No one had the energy or will power this year. Mom said it looked fine. I started to protest that nothing was done right but then stopped when I saw how tired she looked.

The radiation had given her a second wind that was now more like a breeze. All of us were tired and needed a break. I knew, however, that Mom was not going to get any respite from this no matter how long it took.

Her birthday was at the end of January but she didn't make it. When we got the word that the end was near and we were all up in her bedroom, she asked what had happened. She thought someone was hurt. I heard her whisper, "Oh it's time."

She got to do what everyone seems to want to do. She died at home in her bed with her family around her. Even in death she was teaching us by her example.

We had to get the family home ready to sell. There was a ton of stuff to sift through. It was sad and at the same time fun to look at all the things that have made up our lives. She'd kept it all—so many pictures, even old ones from Norway. I wish people had put names and dates on many of them. Too late now as there's no one left to ask.

Thanks Mom, and thank you, God, for allowing me to have the best Mom there ever was.

Griselda Silva-Rivera
MY ABUELITA WAS A FLAPPER

My *Abuelita's* spirit was as wild and wiry as the black hair she tamed daily into a long braid and rolled into a tight neat bun. As a little girl I would watch in amazement as she brushed out that unbridled mane and lacquered it into a giant ebony cinnamon roll that would rest at the nape of her neck. Yet her character was never gooey-sweet like the grandma on the box of See's Candy.

Besides recipes for *Mole de Olla*, there were many lessons learned in that humble kitchen and it is there where I came to understand her quest for freedom and love for this country. As this Fourth of July approaches, it is because of *Abuelita* that I know how blessed I am to be an American and that we must never take for granted the liberties and privileges we possess.

It is only now that I appreciate the resiliency *Abuelita* instilled in me through her tough love and no nonsense attitude. Her birth in 1906 coincided with the incubation of a festering revolt against Porfirio Diaz' brutal dictatorship in Mexico. Her home town, Aguililla, Michoacan, to this day remains a hot bed of violence, and those who originate from *tierra caliente* are notorious for their sulfurous dispositions. That was *Abuelita's* personality in a nutshell. I once attempted to roll my eyes at her in my misguided preteen rebellion, but I quickly willed my gaze back into submission. Nevertheless, she left my birthday present on the top shelf of our closet staring down at me for an entire year and admonished me daily for showing disrespect to my elders.

Lessons learned from *Abuelita* were swift, mighty, and memorable. While my parents toiled endlessly in search of the "American Dream," she remained the pillar of our extended household. It would never have occurred to me to challenge *Abuelita's* form of discipline or advice. Each day I live only confirms the veracity of her many statements such as, "Laziness is a mortal sin." There were many who perhaps came to resent her seriousness and her apparent "glass half empty" attitude toward life.

When *Abuelita* described how her widowed Mama Chuche would kneel for hours in front of the *metate** grinding cocoa beans and cinnamon into sugary cakes, I began to understand her yearning for freedom and justice. My grandmother never made it past the first grade due to *Presidente Porfirio's* efforts to extinguish any seed of knowledge, faith and hope by shooting at those who tried to go to school and church. Yet Great Grandma Chuche and her young family precariously made their way each Sunday to take refuge in the arms of our *Virgencita* and ask her to intercede with Papa Dios to bring an end to the chaos.

A mother's desperation to keep her children alive compelled Mama Chuche to make that arduous train ride to a quiet pocket of paradise to wait out the revolution in Santa Barbara, California. After spending nearly a decade working and planning a return to Aguililla, the Roaring Twenties came into full swing. *Abuelita*, now a teenager, had tasted freedom, and the idea of returning to Michocan was out of the question. Ironically, while the revolution against Pofirio's rule had finally ended, the rebellion in Mama Chuche's only daughter had just begun. In protest, my *Abuelita* took a pair of sewing shears and butchered her hair into an unsophisticated bob.

Abuelita's defiance and unwillingness to leave the United States were met with stern resistance. Her severed braid remained motionless on the floor like a defeated snake, but still her insubordination resurrected with a vengeance when she took on the most unladylike habit of smoking. She clung to the persona of a flapper in an attempt to stake claim to her freedom. Yet when she saw that her tactics were failing, my *Abuelito* Joaquin, twenty-five years her senior, offered her an easy ticket to what she presumed would be freedom.

Sadly, *Abuelita*, her husband, and young family of three were repatriated to Mexico during the Depression. In the mid-sixties she was finally able to come back to the United States and escape the ensnarement of her marriage, after dutifully raising her youngest child. Even after a diagnosis of terminal lung cancer, she dismissed criticisms and diligently studied for her citizenship at the age of ninety-four. I never once questioned her efforts because I understood her lifelong search for freedom. Sadly, *Abuelita* died before becoming a citizen. I have come to realize that her final lesson was as passionate and enduring as those of our forefathers who declared our independence.

metate is a slab of volcanic rock slab and rolling pin used to grind maize or other foods.

Mike Orton

THE OTHER SIDE

Paralyzed in cold disbelief, I stared into the cavity of an anemic turkey. Mom's new husband, Richard, had reserved a more substantial bird for the *big* table while exiling Sis, Randy, and me to the other side of the dining room. Eight months pregnant, Sis struggled to slide into the chair next to me and nearly sent the old card table crashing. A ghostly tablecloth draped the relic, but I could still see Dad rolling Parcheesi dice over the torn vinyl.

The doorbell rang.

"He's late," Richard announced as he carved the turkey with a surgeon's precision. "Late for Thanksgiving."

Seated dutifully to Richard's right, in the "mother's seat," Mom glanced downward, as if she were still praying—maybe she was.

"Really?" Sis said, looking at the rest of us, and then grunting. "Allow me," as she heaved herself from her chair and waddled to the door; once it opened, Randy burst in with two bottles of wine and a raucous hello. My little bro was a big man, not just in size, but also in demeanor. The more he disliked someone, the more he would feign respect and admiration. After plopping the wine bottles down in front of Richard, he started in.

"Hey Richard, how the heck are you?" he belted.

"Hello, Randy. Have a seat. You're almost on time. You've met my daughters, Alyssa and—"

"Well, yeah! Hey Alyssa," he grinned, vigorously shaking her hand. "How's Pepperdine?"

Her pointy nose tilted up with her eyebrows. "It's fine, I imagine. I graduated from Stanford last year."

"Well yes, of course you did," Randy returned apologetically. "Kudos!" Moving on, he looked to Richard's oldest daughter and her husband. "Denise, you look absolutely stunning tonight. And you sir, how are you doing, Roger?"

"It's Paul," Denise corrected, unamused.

"Darn, I was so close this time," he quipped with a wink.

Mom popped out of her chair as if startled from a sound sleep. She grabbed the wine bottles and put them in the cabinet. "Dinner's ready," she cooed melodically. "Sit over there, next to your sister."

Randy looked over his shoulder and our eyes met. We didn't have to speak. He looked at the big table, dressed in linen with a cornucopia centerpiece surrounded by crystal water glasses. Bright orange napkins rested on Grandma's best china, pulled through the wooden rings we used to use as extra pieces on the old carom-board. Then he looked back to our little table, the basket of pinecones and paper napkins.

"Over here brother, next to me," I said.

The conversation at the big table sounded like a bad episode of *Father Knows Best* with Richard talking about wanting grandkids and asking when Paul would finish his residency.

My brother, sister, and I sat quietly picking at our food. Even Randy retreated into his head. When he looked up, I knew he was hurting, because I was.

"You know," he began haltingly. "There are four sides to this table and only *three* of us. They could have pushed the tables together."

"I suggested that earlier," Sis said, poking a string bean into her mouth with her fingers. "Before you got here."

"What happened?" I asked.

"Richard didn't want to eat with Danny's kids."

"He said that?" My brother and I gasped in unison.

"No," she smiled, directing her gaze at the big table. "He didn't say anything, but that's what I heard."

"And Mom?" I asked.

Sis flicked a stray piece of corn at me, her eyes wide and teasing. "Duh!"

I laughed and launched a string bean missile in her direction. "Don't you 'duh' me!"

"You guys are pathetic," Randy snapped, rolling a ball of stiff mashed potatoes between his fingers.

"That's enough," said Sis. "Don't make them right about us. You wouldn't act that way if Dad was here."

"If Dad was here, he'd be banished to the kiddie table, too," Randy protested, winding up his potato ball for an inter-table launch.

"Wait!" I shouted.

The room became silent and I could feel the eyes from the big table burning on the back of my neck as Randy and Sis looked to see what I would do. "There are four sides to this table," I said softly as I stood, retrieved the last folding chair from the closet, and set it in place. Randy smiled knowingly and headed to the cabinet for the wine. Sis, with more agility than I expected, grabbed another setting.

With our glasses full and arms raised, we toasted our empty space.

"To Thanksgiving," Sis uttered with tearing eyes.

"To the other side," I added.

Randy smiled at Sis and me. "To Dad," he whispered.

Ximena Tagle Ames
THE NEED FOR A TWO-HEADED GOD

January is a dull, hollow, useless month that needs to be named truthfully; it should be called Blah or the Regret month. January is, after all, National Oatmeal month. Very appropriate. It's a gray, cold, miserable month when we add to the misery by making resolutions to improve ourselves. Each one points out our failings. We swear to balance check books, exercise, and be nice to people we can barely tolerate, all the while knowing we won't keep our word.

No wonder January is the month when we hold our breath until we get to February and a chance to eat chocolate. Then it's clear sailing for the rest of the year during which we have holidays galore. But not in January, predictably a month dedicated to regrets. People grumble: I spent too much. I ate too much, and oh, no...no...no. Tell me I didn't say that at the Christmas party. The only distractions to the month are the usual predictions.

This year, however, may be dull by comparison. How can 2013 compete with 2012 and The End of the World? Who would have dreamed after all the documentaries, the movie, the NASA hotline to handle calls from petrified citizens that when the fearsome day arrived, 12-21-2012, it would be so exceedingly boring? No earthquakes, no meteors, no sun flares. I looked forward to colorful Quetzalcoatl, the half man-half god winged serpent behind the Mayan prophesies, descending from heaven. But it was a zip day, *nada.* No, more terrifying than the prophecies, the world seems to have stayed the same.

On the other hand, January could be the one month when we have time to reflect. Undisturbed by thoughts of parties and food, we can take a moment to be at peace. Consider that the month is named after the Roman god, Janus, a creature with two heads, one that looks forward and one that looks back. As such, Janus invites us to collect memories, like delicate flowers, and press them between the pages of a book to keep their colors fresh. Looking to the future, we can remember that, in spite of the unpredictable nature of life, we can be hopeful, we can chose to face the future with confidence and the security that comes from knowing our own strengths. We can take a minute to reflect on family and friends and be grateful, knowing we have loved ones to rely on.

Janus is also the god of the doorway, symbolic of change, new beginnings, and a path from one place to another. Aside from all the hoopla about the end of the world, the year 2012 was described as the start of a spiritual awakening when humanity would transition from fear and violence to harmony, cooperation, and peace—a hope in the hearts of men for thousands of years. During 2012, we suffered as the killing of innocent women and children escalated in Syria and Afghanistan. In America, we were repulsed by the violence and suffering of three mass shootings. Many felt the need for change, a yearning for decency, compassion, and unity. We are still baffled as to how to accomplish that task, but we are now only at the doorway, at the start. My hope is we will have the courage to step through that doorway to find solutions and improve our tired, battered world.

In January, we can take time to remember happiness is not a constant state of being, but comes in a multitude of fleeting moments: a kiss from a child; the touch of your lover's hand; a glance at the beauty of the stars. Peaceful January could be the month to explore our spirituality, the eternal nature of our true being, and the power of good over evil.

On second thought, January is aptly named. There is something sacred about looking to the past with gratitude and to the future with hope.

Destry Ramey

MY DAD, JACK

Some of us are blessed to have one individual who influences our lives so profoundly that we adopt some of that person's unique qualities to become part of our core values. That individual in my life was my dad, Jack Wingerter.

Daddy was a simple man, the youngest male of thirteen children. He was raised on a farm in a German colony in Bismarck, North Dakota by immigrant German-Russian parents.

Years later, my dad used German, his primary language, to interpret and comfort young prisoners of war as a military police officer during WWII. His quick wit, sense of humor, and optimism radiated from every cell of his body. Memories of his warm smile and contagious laughter, coupled with his teasing and silly jokes, continue to bring a smile to my face—even today. I have no doubt the plight of the young prisoners of war was less of a burden and more tolerable because they knew my dad.

When Daddy was a child, it was expected he would contribute to the support of the family. For this reason, he had to discontinue his education after eighth grade. Even though he didn't have a formal education, what made him unique was that he viewed obstacles as challenges and challenges as opportunities.

If he needed a specific part or tool that was unavailable, he created his own. His gadgets, including his patented "Tyrejac," are part of his legacy. This invention, named by my mother, was a planter created from a tire and rim. Sadly, no royalties were received despite the Tyrejacs popularity during the 1960's. Daddy recycled long before recycling was the norm.

My dad owned and operated a full-service Texaco station for fifty years and was Texaco's longest employee. For this reason, Texaco honored him with a model-sized, pewter Texaco station engraved with his name that he proudly displayed. He embraced his customers and gave them and their cars full service with humor, integrity, and respect.

"When you make someone laugh," Daddy said, "that laughter will have a domino-effect on others throughout the day." His initial priority each day was to make the first person he met laugh.

To daddy a cup was never half-empty; it was always half-full. On one occasion, Daddy was offered a coffee refill. "I'd like just a half cup," he said. "The top half, please." When I noted the baffled expression on the waitress's face and the glint in my dad's eye, I smiled and said, "My father is the ultimate optimist."

Daddy always enjoyed having "tricks up-his-sleeve." One fond childhood memory centered on a visit to his Texaco station. Thinking how smart I was, I mentioned to him that he had accidentally placed one can upside down in the center of his stacked oil can-pyramid display. He just smiled and remarked, "It got your attention, didn't it? If they were all the same, nobody would notice."

My dad worked hard to provide for his family because they were everything to him. Children were attracted to him like steel to a magnet, eager to be included in his good-natured teasing. Our yard was a welcome playground for family and friends. Daddy provided multiple, fun-filled activities including badminton, croquet, volleyball, and tetherball. He loved to play horseshoes and was an excellent bowler. I recall many trophies lining his office shelves.

Daddy always made time for his family, friends, church, or anyone who needed his assistance. He took pride in his perfectly manicured lawn and mowed it almost daily. In later years, shadowed by Bruno, his beloved six-pound poodle, cutting the lawn became his primary exercise.

During those later years, he was challenged by Parkinson's disease. It was difficult for him to speak or move. He was happiest when his family was present and his wife of more than fifty years was nearby.

Forever ingrained in my heart was the day my dad and I were sitting together in the senior home where he lived. Speech and ambulation were difficult for him and Parkinson's had dulled his facial expressions. Sitting in his wheelchair, he gingerly turned to me and asked clearly without his usual slurred speech, "Was I a good father?"

"Oh, yes, Daddy, you were the best," I responded. I gave him a big hug. "You are the best Dad ever!"

Unable to smile, he turned away. I saw peace, comfort, and moisture in his bright blue eyes, the bluest of eyes I will forever remember.

Kalila Volkov
KENTUCKY FRIED CHRISTMAS

Celebrating Christmas in Kentucky sounded as odd to me as watching a frail, elderly woman ride a skateboard. I was accustomed to our family tradition of being home for the holidays in New England. But in 1978 I was a young college kid whose parents were recently divorced, and I no longer had the same home to return to. That Christmas I felt exposed and vulnerable as I began looking at life in new ways: as the grown child who had left the nest; as the young woman with parents living in separate states; as a guest in Mom's new Kentucky home with her changing holiday customs; and as a semi-stranger to my aunts and cousins whom I barely knew. I was aware of Southern hospitality, but I didn't expect to be so surprised by this group of jovial women who gave me a Southern-style Christmas I would never forget.

What made this Christmas sparkle in my memory was that my grown relatives did *not* act like mature adults. My cousin suggested that we take a little drive to see the house that was annually adorned with a huge lighted Elvis placard on the rooftop. Snow had only dusted the town but we still needed to bundle up from the cold. Piling into the car, just before dusk on Christmas Eve, we drove across town to gawk at the gaudy celebrity decoration. Elvis was depicted in his typical pose—standing with legs apart, knees bent, and microphone in hand—and bright blinking bulbs surrounded his image.

My aunts were such a lively bunch, they decided we should stand on the sidewalk by the house and sing one of Elvis's tunes, "Blue Christmas." The five of us belted out the refrain with plenty of twang and dramatics. We had only made it through the first chorus when the front door swung open and out popped a young boy of about twelve. Our singing group promptly snuffed out our giggles when we noticed the boy in the doorway was holding a shotgun! He made it clear by moving it in our direction that we should end our taunting display immediately. Aghast but still chuckling, we dashed away and finished another chorus in the car. As we drove through the neighborhoods and gazed at the colorful Christmas displays, I felt awkward about poking fun at the tacky Elvis fans. On the other hand, the cheery presence of these women comforted me. Being a young adult, I hadn't yet read any Southern women authors, so I didn't fully appreciate what a "hoot" these folks were, but I admired the spunk and sassiness which seemed to be an essential part of their characters.

The festive tone continued through the evening as company came and went from my aunt's house. Fortified with lots of sugar and a little alcohol, we revelers agreed to stay up late and attend Midnight Mass. The hush and reverence within the glowing sanctuary filled me with peace and a joyful expectation of Christmas Day. Our row of merry ladies sat piously for the ceremony up until Holy Communion. At that point I became aware that there was a disturbance in our pew for it seemed to be rocking or shaking. I glanced toward my aunts and cousins and discovered my second big surprise that Christmas Eve. They were all cracking up with laughter in church! Some were bowing their heads to quiet the laughing, while others were leaning against one another to stifle the noise. My mom couldn't contain herself enough to tell me the joke, but I found myself suffering with both a sore face and cramped belly from laughing so hard as the intense hilarity spread among us. I could hardly wait for the mass to end so I could discover what had caused the ruckus.

It turned out that one of my aunts had asked my mom if she would be taking Communion. My mom, not the religious type but with a "Ya-Ya Sisterhood" personality, whispered, "I'm so full I couldn't eat another bite."

These Southern women knew how to live it up, and they also had that inherent ability to liven things up. Being silly came naturally to these gals who greeted the magical holiday season with open amusement and childlike wonder. It was that year I realized that even though I had become a more mature adult, I could become an elated kid all over again at Christmastime.

Edward J. Longstreth

JUST CALL ME JIM

The stormy skies added to the gloom on the day he left. I was nineteen years old and standing in the hallway of my grandparents' apartment. My brother walked over and softly uttered, "I'm so sorry, Eddie, but Grandpa passed away a few minutes ago." I looked away and quickly wiped my tears as I began to remember my time with Grandpa.

It was 1976 and another hot day in Carrolton, Texas. I was five years old and wiggling with excitement. Once a week Grandpa took me to check for missing or unlatched locks at the self-storage facility that he and my Grandma managed. This was after my nap, which was mostly spent attempting to sneak peanut butter from the office pantry and waiting. Finally the time came. Grandpa repeated his textbook instructions in a way that only Grandpa could.

"Let's go check those locks, Eddie. Now, you remember what to do if you see a door with no lock?"

"Of course, that's when I sound the silent alarm." This consisted of flailing about while trying to stay quiet.

"That's right, Eddie, and what do you do if you see a door with an unlatched lock?"

"I scream as loud as possible. That's my favorite part, Grandpa."

"Are you sure you're up for it, Eddie? Can I trust you to make a really loud sound?"

"I won't let you down, Grandpa, I promise."

I can't remember ever going on our rounds without seeing at least one or more doors without a lock and always an unlatched one at the end of our ride. Of course, I flailed my arms when appropriate and hollered up a storm the instant an unlatched lock presented itself. Grandpa had me push the locks shut while warning me, "I'm responsible for customer security. My job is in your hands, Eddie." I still wonder if Grandpa unlatched those locks during my naps.

When driving in the car with Grandma, she would complain about his driving. Once she screamed, "Jim, Jim, you're driving too fast!"

As usual, he replied, "Margaret, I'm driving as best I can, just let me drive, woman!" After a few moments, Grandma and I noticed Grandpa had slowed down to half the freeway speed limit.

"Jim, Jim, you're driving too slow; you need to pick it up," Grandma shouted.

"I'm just tryin' to drive slow enough to keep you happy while keeping the boy safe," Grandpa said with a grin. I giggled at his sarcastic humor.

I hadn't seen him in three years when I received word that he wasn't doing well. I took the first flight from California to Texas. Thank God, I was able to spend a few hours with him before he died. He told me his favorite story one last time.

"I was the youngest of thirteen kids and they didn't know what to call me, so they just called me every name they could think of. My name is William, Henry, Walter, Sam…Ruben, Rufus, Solomon, Jim…. Mcthaniel, Daniel, Abraham…Roger, Fredrick, Peter, Sam…Simon, Limon, Nicholas, Pat, Christopher, Dick, and Josephat.

"But, when they hollered from the porch to let me know dinner was ready, everybody on the block came a runnin'. So they decided to just call me Jim."

The last thing he said to me was, "I love you, Eddie."

Back at the apartment the tears returned. My brother nodded at me and said, "Keep your chin up; it'll be okay."

I walked outside to be alone with my sadness. The windy skies were shadowed by slow churning clouds. I looked up when I heard the crackle of thunder. *Grandpa is gone and I'll never see him again. I've lost him forever.* My eyes were overflowing with tears when all of a sudden the skies parted as though God was opening Heaven's doors to the earth below. Rays of sunlight flooded my face as locusts chirped softly. I was inundated with peace. In an instant, all of my pain went away. In that moment, I knew my Grandpa was okay.

As quickly as it happened, the clouds returned to blot out the sun. He hadn't left me. He had just moved into a new place while continuing to live within my heart. I'll never forget the kindness he showed me. Grandpas are fathers, too, and my grandpa named, "Just call me Jim" will never be forgotten.

Mary Redmond

I'LL TAKE A BAKER'S DOZEN

Now that revelries have rung and resolutions likely broken, it's tempting to slip into the post-holiday blues. As we head back to the old work-a-day grind, we need look no further than the crisp sky above to relieve that looming sense of winter melancholy. Behold in the night sky a gift, for in this new year of 2012, not twelve but thirteen moons will appear. Just like that extra donut in the celestial pink pastry box called the New Year, Zeus has tossed in an extra. So why not take this opportunity to get reacquainted with our closest neighbor—no astronomy class, calories, or credit cards required.

On January eighth, both the scientifically and romantically inclined will join together and gaze with abandon into the heavens at the first of thirteen full moons in 2012. Not until 2015 will we again enjoy our glowing orb in full splendor this many times within a calendar year. And now that the eight maids have finished their milking, the notion of this many full moons in a single year is guaranteed to send any respectable cow a-leaping. You can join in the lunar spectacle by visiting www.farmersalmanac.com, enter your location, and you will see the exact date and time each full moon will appear.

As the year progresses and the dog days of summer arrive, our enjoyment will reach a crescendo when two full moons appear in August. The first moon will come into sight on the first and the second can be viewed on the thirty-first. Keep in mind that two full moons in a single month is not by *Farmer's Almanac* standards, a blue moon. By definition, a blue moon is the extra full moon in a season when that season has four full moons. Therefore, strictly speaking, our next true "blue moon" won't appear until August 2013. And yes, it's confusing enough to set even Zeus' dog a-howl.

Of course myths associated with the full moon are as countless as the gods in the Greek heaven. Within those blue veins of myth runs the perennial favorite fable that NASA's moon landings were simply an expensive hoax complete with cinematic-style effects. Most notably, in 1971, also a year with thirteen full moons, Alan Shepard, while brandishing a six iron, drove a golf ball down the lunar fairway of the ol' man's celestial face. This is a ruse that we can only hope NASA didn't have time to coordinate.

Even Wall Street is not immune to loony mythical spells or the siren call to a moon made of a wholly different kind of green. The authors of *Lunar Cycle Effects in Stock Returns*, while using all the major U.S. stock indices over the past 100 years, determined that returns in the fifteen days around new moon dates are about double the returns in the fifteen days around full moon dates. If the whipsaw markets of 2011 weren't enough, this study could certainly send weary investors running to the nearest lunar links for a vigorous round of golf— thirteen times.

Finally, for the romantic in all of us, Chinese folklore spins the tale of Yue-Laou, the old man in the moon. A heavenly being responsible for the sole task of joining predestined lovers in a rather permanent way. While those of us in the west are celebrating an extra moon under the Gregorian calendar, many people around the world will be celebrating the extra moon phase under the lunisolar calendar. The beginning of the lunisolar calendar is January 23rd, commonly known as Chinese New Year. This new cycle will begin the year of the dragon and is celebrated as a symbol of luck and vitality. You can bet that a little good fortune and verve will go a long way when a man in the moon is choosing your life mate.

NASA to Wall Street, Beijing to San Luis, our world is connected by myth and by fact to that glorious ball in the nighttime sky. Luckily we don't have to travel far in this part of the country to escape the din of city lights, a place where we can gaze up into a clear winter night, at the myth and majesty of our closest neighbor.

Ximena Tagle Ames

FELIZ NAVIDAD

It was going to be the worst Christmas ever. I was fourteen years old and sure the holidays would make my miserable life even worse. Mother and my little sister, The Brat, decorated the tree, but I stayed in my room, listening to Los Quinteros, Chile's most famous singers, thinking about all the things I didn't like about America. No, I didn't like it, not one little bit, and I really hated my mother for bringing us here.

Nothing made any sense after my father died, least of all our coming to America. But Mother didn't care. All she wanted was a job so we wouldn't have to live with Grandmother and she could be independent, whatever that meant. She also didn't care that I was miserable at school. "How do you pronounce your name?" the teacher asked. "Is it Eczema?"

I wanted to scream. "I'm not a skin condition."

But the misery didn't end there, oh, no.

"You need to be my little helper," Mom said shortly after we got settled in. "Let me teach you how to cook."

How could she be so mean? In Chile, Dominguita cooked delicious empanadas for us and we sat at a long, mahogany table set with china and silverware. Here we ate on paper plates.

"I don't want to be the cook."

She didn't even hear me, just poured water into a pot and went on with her lesson. "All you need to know," she said, "is how to boil water. Now you can cook rice, spaghetti, hard boiled eggs, everything." Mother smiled brightly, as if she had given me the secret to eternal happiness.

"But I don't like hard boiled eggs." I slumped into a chair.

"If just for the holidays, Ximena, could you smile a little? And please, be nice to your sister."

I stared at The Brat, who sat on the sofa picking her nose. Oh, joy. Just what I wanted to do, spend time with The Brat. I missed my friends and my ten zillion cousins who kept me from ever, ever getting lonely. In America, lonely was all I knew.

Lonely and cold. Why did people want a white Christmas anyway? Snow made my nose red and earmuffs made me look silly. In Chile, Christmas marked the start of summer. I loved to spend the whole summer with all my cousins, swimming, horseback riding, and best of all, eating peaches right off the trees. I wasn't going to get any peaches this year. Mother said they were too expensive. I was going to have to be happy with canned ones. This is what I had to look forward to: Christmas, lonely, cold, and eating canned peaches.

When the dreaded day arrived, Mother plugged in the lights on the tree. She made spaghetti for lunch, and after we ate we began to open our presents.

The Brat came over to where I was sitting and snuggled in next to me. She gave me a card made of beige construction paper. I saw she had carefully printed my name in pink crayon across a blue sky.

"I told the kids at school that your name is easy to pronounce," she said. "Just pretend the *x* is an *h*, I told them. Easy."

I stared at the card. A big yellow sun rose over snow-covered mountains. At the bottom of the page, she had drawn a row of peach trees, just like home. Under them, in large block letters, she wrote, "*Feliz Navidad.*" I felt a funny sensation in my nose, and for a weird moment I thought I was going to cry.

Mother's gifts were practical: socks and underwear. Oh, joy. Then they handed me a large box. It was heavy so I guessed it was a pair of shoes, probably something waterproof and ugly. I put it down next to me on the floor. Maybe I could go to my room now.

"Go on, open it," they said and put the box on my lap.

I pried it open and gasped. The box was full of oranges, figs, grapes, and six yellow peaches, all marked, "Product of Chile."

"Maybe now you won't be so sad," Mother said. She kissed me on the forehead.

"*Gracias, Mamacita, gracias.*"

The Brat hugged me and I was surprised at how nice her soft cheek felt against mine. She gave me a big, sloppy kiss that I just had to wipe off my face. Then I threw my arms around her.

"I... I...I love you," I whispered.

"Merry Christmas," she said and took off dancing around the room. "*Feliz Navidad!*"

Paul Alan Fahey

THE CHRISTMAS SPY

On December 24, 1938, I was ten years old and found myself at Southampton Harbor, along with forty other passengers wrapped in coats, scarves, and hats, waiting to board the magnificent "flying boat," the Dixie Clipper.

Father sent me to England at the end of summer to spend several months with his older brother, Bertie. I'd talked Father into a round-trip steamship ticket from New York, but with rumors of the Brits on the verge of a hellish war with Germany, he cabled Bertie to send me home early.

Inside the clipper, green curtains hung from brass rods over small, oblong windows, and each compartment contained four to six recliners upholstered in brown velvet.

I wasn't seated long before a woman wearing a gray suit and a red tam took the chair next to mine. Even to a ten-year-old, she looked swell: creamy complexion, wavy blond hair, and hazel eyes. "My first name's Marantha," she said, with a faint, foreign accent. "My last is much harder to pronounce. You can call me Miss M, if you like."

I told her I was Harold Davenport, the third, and then jumped a bit as a loud bang reverberated through the cabin.

"Just the door closing, love." She adjusted a sprig of holly on the lapel of her jacket, and then showed me how to properly buckle my seat belt.

As the clipper roared to life, Miss M reached over and held my hand while the plane soared heavenward and eventually leveled off at cruising altitude. "I'm positive Britain will declare war in the next few months, Harold. What do you think?"

I told her about the military trucks I'd seen passing on the road near my uncle's estate and the tension in the stores whenever I accompanied our cook into the village. About here I decided to have some fun. I pointed to a fellow dressed in a white suit and Panama hat. "Do you see that man up ahead?"

Miss M nodded.

"He's probably a spy traveling with a fake identity."

"And passing secrets to his accomplice on the plane," she said, laughing and apparently enjoying the game.

I was a little nervous about flying over what Bertie called, "all that water," and asked her about our route.

She opened her purse and pulled out a piece of paper with dates and times written in dark ink. "We're scheduled to stop at Foynes in Ireland, then nothing till after the crossing. A place called Whiskey Bay in Newfoundland."

Christmas morning in Whiskey Bay. I imagined brownish-yellow foam lapping at the shore, a town full of merry inhabitants.

We stopped briefly in Ireland, and when we were again aloft, the steward served dinner. Later, Miss M went to the bar and brought back a warm mug of eggnog. "This will help you sleep, Harold," and then she asked the steward for blankets and pillows.

I listened to the steady drone of the engines, the whir of the propellers, and after finishing my drink, I fell into a deep sleep.

In the morning, I woke fuzzy and disoriented. I turned to see how Miss M had passed the night, but found her chair empty. I asked the steward where she'd gone.

"The lady got off at Whiskey Bay," he said. "She didn't want to wake you."

I had a vague memory of being jostled and bumped about, then later someone's lips brushing my cheek. I couldn't believe I'd slept through the early morning landing.

"She seemed to know one of the gents up front," the steward said. "They left together."

"Not the man in the white suit?" I wondered why this came to mind.

"Right. That's the one."

My thoughts were a jumble. *Whiskey Bay…All that talk of spies. If she was traveling with that man, why did she sit with me?* I reached inside my coat pocket for the small package Uncle had given me. "For your father," he'd said. "Guard it carefully."

The package was gone.

Father met me at the Port Washington dock, and though I was glad to be home, I couldn't stop thinking of Miss M. There were so many unanswered questions.

****

I have been lucky in life, more fortunate than most, with plenty of time and money to indulge my whims. For years I dreamt of midnight flights, of silver gliding over water, and rarefied air, thick with mystery.

In my late sixties, these images led me back to the past and to a remote spot on the Newfoundland coast. There in a small churchyard overlooking Whiskey Bay was a headstone, bent by the wind and facing the Atlantic. Just a name on a piece of slate.

And the name was MARANTHA.

Tom Harrington

CHRISTMAS SKIS

Winter storms careened off Lake Erie into the bucolic country crossroads of Belle Valley where my family lived in the house my father built. They brought sleet and hail and sometimes billows of snow. We kids loved it when snowdrifts and cold turned the landscape into a winter playground. We longed for extra days off from school and for Christmas vacation to begin.

Sleds, skates, toboggans and snow saucers tumbled out of garages and barns, as country kids dusted off their favorites and converged to whiz down snow-packed hills and across ponds. Some of the best sites were near our house, so my brothers and I became proficient with toboggans and sleds early on. But I dreamt of skiing.

I don't know where the idea came from. We were blue-collar Scotch-Irish, not Nordic school children who skied through picturesque villages. It was 1955. Television had not landed in our household yet, so I must have seen an elf skiing across the front of a Christmas card. It was a dream from some far off culture.

While sleds and snow saucers were at every hardware and country store, skis didn't enter storekeepers' inventories or fit our Presbyterian frugality. I dropped snowstorms of ski hints. We didn't have the "ask Santa clause" in our family Christmas tradition. Gifts were performance and budget-based, so I applied myself to gaining special merit by outworking my brothers. We kept the driveway cleared for our breadwinner so he could drive to work at the locomotive factory. Materializing skis was not easy labor.

In the meantime, I contented myself with sledding, or joining my cousins to get towed behind my mischievous uncle's car over icy country roads. Long strings of kids on sleds would trail behind the car clinging to one another's feet for dear life. Even bathed in exhaust fumes, I dreamt of skis, but I saw no clues of my good intentions being rewarded.

Encouraged by my eighth-grade shop teacher and *Popular Mechanics* magazine, I decided to make my own skis. I mentioned the idea to my mom and dad and got the "Go ahead, make your own skis" reply. "You can use your paper route money." Tempered encouragement was part of our family code.

Undaunted, I got the wood at school, cut two planks, and planed them to the right shape and thickness from tip to tail. Unfortunately, my parents' permission was insufficient for my success. There was an unforeseen hot water problem.

Our family had just evolved from heating water in a coal burning potbelly stove in the basement to an electric hot water heater. Constant hot water for bending skis made baths or hot running water in the kitchen impossible. My mother wasn't ready to return to heating dishwater in a teakettle on the stove, so my dad helped me plumb a bypass on the abandoned coal water heater. As long as I fed the potbelly stove, I could use all the hot water I needed.

I talked my mom into tending the stove when I was at school. At night I tiptoed from my unheated attic room to the basement to mind the steaming and bending. Before long, I decided it was easier just to sleep on the basement stairs with steam and the coal stove to keep me warm. It reminded me of Saturday saunas in town where my father and I sat with a bunch of towel-wrapped old men, grunting their opinions while shrouded in steam clouds and cigar smoke.

I wanted skis by Christmas so I could thrill my friends with graceful arcs across the hill. The wood was bent and varnished but I couldn't find or make bindings to work with my country-boy galoshes. Christmas came and went without me becoming a ski hero. I was the heartbroken owner of two shapely strips of wood. I hid them under my bed.

The next Christmas was not a time of high expectations. We normally got practical gifts like socks, underwear, a shirt, school supplies, and more tracks for the family train set.

Christmas morning, still in warm pajamas, I opened the door at the bottom of the attic stairs and looked across our living room. I was amazed. Next to our homegrown Christmas tree was a pair of shiny store-bought skis, with real bindings, and a pair of used ski boots. I scrambled to put them on and just stood there on the rug imagining my first downhill run. Last year's determination had merited opening the family purse strings.

My skiing dream propelled me to the snowy Atlas Mountains in Africa, where camels pulled skiers uphill, to resorts in the Alps, and fabled ski mountains in North America.

Griselda Silva-Rivera
A NEW YEAR'S RESOLUTION

Cuando él Nacio, La Paz Vino—When He was Born, Peace Came—reads the inscription on a very prized 2004 Hispanic ornament that I just had to have as I shot through the card shop that sweltering September afternoon. It's ironic that on this chilly January morning of 2005 I wasn't feeling much peace in my life as I haphazardly rushed to remove all my treasured Latino decorations from the Christmas tree. I plucked off everything from hand painted *jarritos*—miniature ceramic Mexican dishes, *chilitos*—chile ornaments, and, of course, those pricey Hispanic ornaments.

I hurried to get my precious collection off this dried-up fire hazard, so that I could drag it to the street and beat the city garbage truck when it made its annual Christmas tree pickup. I made it just in time.

Afterward, as I plopped down on the couch, I began to think seriously about my New Year's resolution. This time I promised myself I was going to give up my biggest temptation—*chicharrones*! I toyed with the idea of abandoning fried pork rinds once and for all. I desperately needed the health change.

My doctor said all the factors indicated I needed to bring my cholesterol level down. I knew I was a middle-aged Latina, who was pleasantly plump, more than slightly under-active, and dependent on blood pressure medication. Yet, I wondered whether it was realistic to even attempt to give up *chicharrones*, since I was convinced that I had a genetic predisposition to the addiction that came from my maternal *abuelita's* side.

I rationalized the whole situation there on the couch among the scattered pine needles. *Hey, if Abuelita lived to be ninety-four eating chicharrones, then they can't be all that bad for you.*

I began to get a cozy nostalgic feeling as I recalled our mutual love for *chicharrones*, and our crazy trips to the dentist after *Abuelita* had busted the teeth from her dentures because she stubbornly refused to give up those deep-fried delicacies. I comforted my conscience by remembering how *Abuelita* died of old age, and not clogged arteries. Then I reflected on how different and simply she lived her life. Most of the other foods she ate were rarely over-processed or taken in excess. She worked hard and within reason. She led a balanced life of rest, family, and prayer.

I rethought my resolution for the following year long and hard. I began to see that eating *chicharrones*, being a shop-a-holic, drinking too much, smoking, or any bad habits we aspire to change, are simply symptoms of our unresolved issues. The consequences for the poor choices we make logically result in living an unbalanced life.

In all honesty, the only time I craved greasy pork skins, or had the urge to buy lots of useless stuff was when I was overworked, tired, and hungry. The scary reality being I was a forty-seven-year-old widow with a ten-year-old son to bring up.

I suddenly realized that perhaps I had been over-simplifying the New Year's tradition of pledging to make a significant change and had lost the essence of what is truly important in life. Maybe having the most spectacular Hispanic Christmas decorations in the universe should not be my top priority. For three years my son had wanted to build a gingerbread house, but I had been too busy keeping to my all-Hispanic Christmas. Perhaps by focusing my energies on my son and loved ones, I would have many more memorable and less hectic Christmas holidays.

No, the New Year's resolution is not about *chicharrones* at all, and Christmas has nothing to do with fancy Latino decorations. Years have passed since that frenzied holiday. I have remarried, built several gingerbread houses with my son and new stepchildren, and even lowered my cholesterol in the bargain. The tranquility and joy of learning to keep things uncomplicated have been priceless. I now realize that life changes and holiday celebrations are about the simple fact that the search for peace begins within yourself and among your loved ones.

Michelle Greer

THE FIRST THANKSGIVING

It's been months since we heard the news, but this Thanksgiving will be the first time our family gathers since the passing of June, our matriarch.

As far back as I can remember, Thanksgiving and all major holidays meant going to Grandma's house—which is probably why I can't picture anything else when I hear that old song, *Over the river and through the woods…* I'm sure you know the rest.

As I walk up those old porch steps now, it feels wrong, hollow. I know if she were here, Grandma would be standing at this very spot, welcoming us to her home. Her eyes would be wide with wonder at how much each of us had grown since the last time we saw her; her arms would be spread wide to fold us into her heart.

I find myself frozen on the porch, watching the swaying of the summer citrus trees in the coastal breeze. It's the sight of my sister in the doorway that finally pulls me forward. We need each other today, and I know we will stay within arm's length the entire time we are in her house.

The front sitting room has the aura of dust and mildew. Clearly no one has been here since May. We walk carefully across the oriental rugs and original wooden floors, carefully because the room feels preserved like an exhibit in a museum. To disturb anything would be to banish the last of her presence.

Despite the overwhelming feeling of unease, I can't keep myself from stroking the exposed keys of her old grand piano as I walk by. I see myself as a child sitting on that bench, my feet swinging, unable to touch the ground. Her hands dance beside mine as she teaches me the simple songs I still remember how to play: "Hot Cross Buns," "Twinkle, Twinkle Little Star," and "Jingle Bells" for the Christmas visits. One of the only things I noticed, as she got older, was how her hands got more and more shaky. The only time she could keep them steady was when she played the piano for us. I can still remember the broad smile she wore as her hands danced over the keys. We applauded as if she were playing in Carnegie Hall, not in her sitting room.

We move out to the garden, and I can't help but smile. Here one of her greater passions in life has survived her loss. She tended her garden with the same love and care that she tended to her family. Hers was a garden that I used to imagine—when I was really little—would take me to a fairy kingdom, because it looked like it could have popped right out of the pages of my storybooks. As I got older, I fancied that it was a bit like the *Secret Garden* that Burnett wrote about. Beyond the patio and the flowerbeds, there is a grassy area where a gargantuan tree was our home base for all games of hide and seek. The tree is boxed in on all sides by a wooden bench, perfect for climbing and seeing every corner of the backyard.

Here is where I find my family, sitting silently in the shade of Grandma June's tree. They sit in solace, holding their glasses of wine as if they were props in a play of a real Thanksgiving. The whole scene feels stilted because the heart of our family is no longer here to guide us.

I pick up a glass with a splash of red wine and raise it to the sky, toward the leaves of the old oak, and I say, "Something is missing this Thanksgiving, someone very special to us all. Grandma June should be sitting right here, smiling at everyone, loving everyone, and reminding us that this is the best day of her life."

Every holiday she would insist that it was. My eyes brim with tears, but I have to smile. I close my eyes and imagine I am standing by her grave, which sits on a peaceful slope of emerald grass beneath a tall oak much like the one I stand beside now. I feel her presence in that beautiful, peaceful spot as much as I feel it here, in her garden, and in her home. A single icy tear falls from my eye. I know that her resting place feels like home to her, and for this I give thanks.

CONTRIBUTORS NOTES

Christine Ahern is currently working on a young adult trilogy. At the 2013 Central Coast Writers' Conference, she won the Lillian Dean Award for Young Adult Fiction. Christine has had several short stories published, including one that won first place in the magazine *Beginnings*. Two of her stories were anthologized in the book *The Worlds Shortest Stories of Love and Death*. Her mainstream novel, *Connie and Monique's Power Trip*, is available as an e-book.

Anne R. Allen is a well-known blogger and the author of seven comic mystery novels, including the bestselling Camilla Randall Mysteries. She's also a published poet. Her blog, Anne R. Allen's Blog, with Ruth Harris, was named one of the "Best 101 Websites for Writers" by *Writers Digest*. She has traveled the world, but is now happily rooted in lovely, foggy Los Osos, CA.

Joe Amaral is a paramedic who spends most of his time spelunking around the California Central Coast. His poetry and short stories have appeared in awesome places around the world, including *A Handful of Dust, Arcadia Magazine, Carcinogenic Poetry, Diverse Voices Quarterly, Kind of a Hurricane Press, Litro, RED OCHRE LiT, Taj Mahal Review,* and *Underground Voices*.

Ximena Tagle Ames was born in Santiago, Chile, and came to the United States in 1954. After receiving a Masters in Counseling from Pacifica Graduate Institute, she had a private practice and retired in 2001. Since then, she has returned to her love of writing, winning several prizes for her poetry. She lives in Nipomo, California.

Darryl Armstrong is a local mortgage banker with the company, *imortgage*. When not writing or helping clients with mortgages, he and his wife, Carol, are usually walking on the beach in Avila where they live. Originally from Bradenton Florida, Darryl graduated from University of South Florida in Tampa. He served in the U.S. Navy from 1964 to 1968. His writing genres of preference are humor and historical fiction.

Mary Martin Benton resides in rural Visalia, California, and is the author of four novels: *Dulsey, Winds of Time, Plain Molly,* and *Bernetta*. Two short stories appear in the anthology, *Leaves from the Valley Oak*. She is a member of the Visalia/Exeter Writers, SLO NightWriters, and Central Coast and San Joaquin Sisters in Crime. Mary's books are available at the Book Garden in Exeter, California, Amazon.com, and Kindle.

Judith Bernstein is a free-lance writer of poetry, non-fiction, and memoir. Her travel articles have been published in *Oregon Coast Magazine* and *Oregon Getaway Guide*. Articles on the arts, lifestyle, the environment, sustainable living, family, and food have appeared in *Oregon Coast Magazine*, *The Oregonian*, *Jewish Currents*, *The New Times* (San Luis Obispo), *San Luis Obispo Tribune*, *Edible SLO Magazine*, Santa Lucia Sierra Club Chapter newsletter, *Dance Magazine*, *African Arts Magazine*, and *The (Portland) Tribune*.

Lillian Brown is a retired community newspaper reporter and editor, public relations specialist, and Cal Poly journalism product, who returned to the Central Coast in 2005. She is exploring the process of creating short stories, poetry, personal essays, and attempting to focus on an historical novel. She leads a NightWriters critique group in the North County, and has numerous published nonfiction articles to her credit.

Willy Bruijns is a retired publishing executive, transplanted first from The Netherlands, and later from the greater L.A. area to the beautiful Central Coast. Willy spends her time traveling, writing, and long-distance running. In her writing she likes to explore the strengths and weaknesses that make us—and her characters—human.

Dawn Cerf is a former CPA turned writer, who began by researching, writing, and publishing family stories and genealogy. She became passionate about helping Liu Yu tell her amazing story in the book they co-authored, *Awakening the Sleeping Tiger: The True Story of a Professional Chinese Athlete*. She has been taking Liu Yu's tai chi classes for twenty years and has traveled to China with her three times.

Andrea Chmelik is a blogger and a stay-at-home mom. She blogs about challenges of parenthood, but also comments on other topics, sometimes seriously, but mostly with humor. Her blog posts were featured at BlogHer.com and published in *Babble's "Best of Blogs, Parenting Uncensored"* e-book series. Andrea was born and raised in Slovakia. After living in New York, Colorado, and Utah, she settled on the Central Coast of California with her husband, son, daughter, and two cats.

Sherry Eiselen is a lifelong Californian with an M.S. from the University of San Francisco. Her first publication was a work of non-fiction, *The Human Side of Child Care Administration*. Since happily retiring to the Central Coast, Eiselen has concentrated on fiction. She is a member of SLO NightWriters and Rough Writers of Cambria. Three novels are currently available on Amazon: *Ahead of Time, In A Flash,* and *Runaway/Throwaway.*

Paul Alan Fahey writes for JMS Books. He is the author of the *Lovers and Liars* series and the editor of the 2013 Rainbow Award-winning anthology, *The Other Man: 21 Writers Speak Candidly About Sex, Love, Infidelity, & Moving*

On. His first LGBT novella, *The View from 16 Podvale Street* won a 2012 Rainbow Award. He lives on the California Central Coast with his husband, Robert Franks, and a gaggle of shelties. For more information, visit paulalanfahey.com.

David Georgi, Professor Emeritus, retired from teaching after 44 years at Santa Maria High School and CSU, Bakersfield. He currently runs a gardening website based on The Dude from *The Big Labowski*. Check it out at: thegardendude.com. He also teaches how to use trekking poles effectively and maintains polecats.org to spread the word. After several years in a NightWriter critique group, he found his voice for a memoir and is currently working on it.

Ruth Goodnow, sometimes penning as Kate Updike O'Connor, lives, writes, and edits in San Luis Obispo, California. Her works of poetry and creative nonfiction have appeared locally in *Lynx Eye, The Tribune, Women's Press,* and *Tolosa Press,* as well as in the *Los Angeles Times* and *Hotchkiss Magazine.* She is the author of the book, *My Name is Rosie,* written in her dog's voice.

Michelle Greer dedicates her story to the memory of June Ablitt, her great grandmother, who died in May 2013. Michelle currently lives in Oceano, California. She is attending Brandman University and is working toward a teaching credential and a Masters in Psychology. She has been writing since she was in third grade and has been a member of SLO NightWriters for one year. To read more by Greer visit Pluvium.net.

Judythe A. Guarnera, editor of the "nightwriter" column in *Tolosa Press* for five years, and the editor of the NW Anthology, *The Best of SLO NightWriters in Tolosa Press 2009-2013,* has been a frequent winner in the "Lillian Dean Contest" at the Central Coast Writers' Conference and a finalist in the NightWriter Golden Quill annual contest. She has been published in local newspapers and magazines, in three anthologies, and in online journals. Judythe is in the final editing phase of her first novel, *Twenty-Nine Sneezes.* Contact her at: j.guarnera@sbcglobal.net

Tom Harrington has made successful forays into adventures around the world—some ill-conceived. To foment joy now, Tom immerses himself in polishing his dream of writing stories that reveal common threads among us, or wanders aimlessly on beaches and hills with his dog, Ginger, listens to music, and hangs with artists and characters of note. He's a member of SLO NightWriters and the Rough Writers in Cambria, California.

Sharyl Heber is a novelist, screenwriter, poet, and a member of the SLO NightWriters Board of Directors. She has served as director for the NightWriter Golden Quill writing competition and has won awards of her own for prose and poetry at the Central Coast Writers' Conference. One of her short stories was published in the e-literary journal, *The Feathered Flounder,* and her screenplay, *Keepers of the Dream,* rose to upper levels of *Miramax's* first *Project Greenlight.*

Kirsty Jenkins is a horse trainer who studies horse behavior and psychology. She is interested in all animals and the many ways people, individually and collectively, interact with them. Kirsty is also a world wanderer, an avid reader, a foodie, a naturalist, a yoga student, a questioner, and a dreamer. She loves all things creative. Writing is one way she can share her version of the world.

Curt Johnson is a writer and attorney who lives in Grover Beach, California. He writes short fiction and was a contributor, editor, and photographer for three volumes of *Writing from Life,* an anthology published by local writers from 2012 to 2013. His short stories explore the lives of people living near the sea. He has published in numerous Central Coast newspapers, and is a member of SLO NightWriters.

Edward J. Longstreth is a motorcycle-riding surfer and author of short stories, a financial wellness book, *The Joy in Wealth,* and soon to come, an historical fiction novel called, *Wild Canyon.* Ed has been a member of SLO NightWriters and a quirky critique group for the last three years. You can find Ed along with eye-popping picture galleries, a fun video, and short stories at his new website and blog at www.edlongstreth.com

Sue McGinty believes the old adage: a person should follow her dream. After the kids flew the nest and with a yen for beach living, an idea for a mystery series, and a cat who'd never ridden in a car, she left Ontario and headed north to Los Osos on the Central Coast. Her mystery novels include: *Murder in Los Lobos, Murder at Cuyamaca Beach,* and *Murder in Mariposa Bay.* All feature former nun, Bella Kowalski. Contact her at http://www.SueMcGinty.com

Carroll McKibbin is a long-time member and former program director for the SLO NightWriters. When he retired as a Cal Poly professor in 2005, he launched a creative writing career. Since then Carroll has published two books, *Lillian's Legacy* and *Apron Strings,* written 126 articles for magazines and newspapers across the United States, and won two firsts and a fourth in writing contests.

Linda Mills, nearly blind from birth, used the words of others as her gateway to the universe. Eventually she found her own words to communicate her world beyond sight. During the past 35 years, her poetry has been featured in a number of publications around the world and online, first as Linda Trujillo, and more recently as Linda Mills. Now retired, she is able to devote herself to her writing and to travel with her very supportive husband.

Jean Moelter has written many plays, articles, and essays. She often performs her work on local stages and is usually pretty funny. She lives in San Luis Obispo with her family and a high-maintenance dog.

Nancy G. Moore writes short fiction, poetry, and dance criticism. Her most recent essays appear in the Parisian collection, *Feminine Futures—Valentine de Saint-Point—Performance, Dance, War, Politics, and Eroticism.* She works as a tour guide at Hearst Castle in San Simeon, California.

Debby Nicklas continues to enjoy an exciting career in marketing, public relations, and philanthropy. Nicklas has published several travel articles and is fully engaged in writing for her current work as Vice President of Philanthropy for French Hospital Medical Center. A mother of two grown sons, Nicklas lives in San Luis Obispo with her husband Steve and dog Sunny.

Mike Orton is a retired teacher who initially wrote short stories, entertainment articles, and radio copy in his spare time. He received a B.A. in socio-cultural anthropology from UC Irvine and his M.A. in education from Grand Canyon University. Mike discovered a passion for writing screenplays, and in a collaborative venture has won awards with a project called, *Searching for Indie.*

Chris Over, a training instructor at Diablo Canyon, enjoys sharing facts and stories, as is evidenced by his work as a San Luis Obispo Lighthouse and trail docent since 2004. He lives in Paso Robles, California, with his family. The story in the anthology is a true story from his childhood and the first to be published.

CS Perryess writes for teens, reads aloud for anyone who will listen, and teaches middle school English. When he gets a spare minute, he enjoys baking bread, upholstering cars, and playing bass. He lives a fine life in a foggy little town on California's Central Coast, with his wonderful wife Ellen and too many dogs.

Anne Peterson, now raised to the rank of honorary membership, joined SLO NightWriters when she moved to the area. She served as president and newsletter editor, and in whatever capacities she was needed. Her Ana-Nimiti column in the NW newsletter kept members' vocabularies sharp. Anne has written four closet novels and many short stories, a couple of which have been published in periodicals.

Tony Piazza is a mystery writer, film historian, and veteran storyteller renowned for his passion for writing and movies. He is the author of three mystery novels and a non-fiction work. Actor and stand-in for movies and television, Piazza has appeared in such notable films as *Magnum Force* and *The Streets of San Francisco*. He is also a member of Sisters in Crime as well as SLO NightWriters.

Shirley Powell's writing has appeared in local and national newspapers and magazines, including *True Romance, The Cleveland Plain Dealer,* and *National Motorist.* A former Los Angeles School District teacher in Carson, she retired to San Luis Obispo, where her daughter attended Cal Poly. Shirley is active in the Assistance League's Operation School Bell, which provides new school clothes for local needy children. Besides writing and reading, she enjoys traveling, cooking, and walking her dog.

Mike Price, age 62, used to work at Diablo Canyon until he escaped with his sanity and most of his hair. Since retiring, he has travelled the country, volunteered in his community of Grover Beach, researched his family history, and written both serious and light hearted stories. He is the husband of one wife, father of six children, and grandfather of twelve. Many of his funniest stories are inspired by this family.

Destry Ramey is a pediatric nurse practitioner who has dedicated her life to working with children nationally and internationally. Her grandpugs and the children in her practice inspired her to write the pug series, *Adventures of Hunter and Ramona.* Destry is currently working on her fourth book, *The Brown Paper Bag.* Proceeds from her books are donated to Animal Rescue, Children's Literacy, and Ending Poverty Together. Visit the pugs at thepugs.com

Mary Redmond worked for The Walt Disney Company prior to relocating to the Central Coast. Her nonfiction articles were first published by *Tolosa Press* in 2011. Her short story, *Siding Number Two,* won the 2012 coveted Dead Bird Award from Sisters in Crime and later appeared in the literary magazine, *The Stone.* She is currently working on her first literary historical fiction novel under the working title *The Packing House.*

Donna Reese taught English for 33 years in California, where she held the department record for teaching the longest ninth grade poetry unit without parental complaint. At age eight, when Donna heard Kay Starr sing a song about a detour and a muddy road, she understood that the words were about more than road conditions. She decided that with poetry her life would be possible. Donna says she has lived by poems ever since. She resides in Oregon with her partner.

Terry Sanville lives in San Luis Obispo, California, with his artist-poet wife (his in-house editor), and one plump cat (his in-house critic). He writes full time, producing short stories, essays, poems, and novels. His short stories have been accepted by more than 180 literary and commercial journals, magazines, and anthologies, including: the *Picayune Literary Review, The Bitter Oleander, Shenandoah,* and *The MacGuffin.* He was nominated for a Pushcart Prize for his story *The Sweeper.*

Jill Schaefer has lived on California's Central Coast for 35 years. Born and bred in England, Jill and her late German husband emigrated with their three sons from England and Germany in 1974. Check out her website http://home.earthlinkj.net/~schaefer234/ for information and videos on her two memoirs, a travel journal, and an historical novel which is available at Amazon.com.

Anne Schroeder is President-Elect of Women Writing the West. Her short stories and essays have appeared in many print magazines. *Cholama Moon* is her first published novel, set in California's earthquake country in the 1870s. It is available through bookstores, Amazon, and Kindle. The second book of the series, *Maria Ines,* will be released in late 2014. Anne now lives in Southern Oregon with her husband and two Labs. Read more at anneschroederauthor.blogspot.com.

David Schwab, educated as a "Fine Artist" with an emphasis in drawing and painting, has always been creative. He turned to short story writing at the prompting of friends. Writing has opened a new world for him. He has learned how hard and rewarding it is. David has had two short stories published in the *Tolosa Press* publications and one in a collection of Christmas stories on the East Coast. Please contact David at daveschwab@sbcglobal.net

Griselda J. Silva-Rivera is a native of Santa Barbara, California, who has found happiness in the tranquility of the Central Coast. During her more than thirty years in education she took joy in imparting the gift of language to all her students. As a second-language learner, she is forever grateful to those teachers who saw beyond a temporary limitation and gave her the skills to pursue the awesome adventure of writing.

Diane Smith, a California educator, is an award-winning writer of short fiction and nonfiction. A proud member of SLO NightWriters, she has been published by *Haunted Waters Press, Leodegraunce, Modern Serenity,* and *Exemplary English.* When not slaving over a hot computer, Diane reads, paints, and plays (with her dog and flute) at home in the paradise known as the Central Coast.

Anthony Toscano believes that language, in all its forms, is a precious gift that allows human beings to express those emotions that live deep inside our souls. Without language, there can be no friendship. Without friendship, there can be no joy. Anthony lives in Morro Bay, California,

3000 miles from the city of his birth, yet quite close to the bridge inside his story.

Susan Tuttle is the author of the suspense novels *Tangled Webs, Piece by Piece, Sins of the Past, Proof of Identity,* and the *Write It Right: Exercises to Unlock the Writer in Everyone* workbook series. Susan is past president of SLO NightWriters and the Central Coast Chapter of Sisters in Crime. Susan is presently the newsletter editor for both organizations. Find her on LinkedIn, Facebook (susanwriter), Twitter (stuttlewriter), and visit her website/blog, www.SusanTuttleWrites.com.

Anna Unkovich is an award-winning teacher, writer, speaker, and coach. She wrote an Op Ed column entitled *Classroom with a View.* She co-authored a three-volume curriculum guide, *Chicken Soup for the Soul in the Classroom,* and a book, *Caring to Teach, Teaching to Care.* Anna authored an e-book of tips and stories for educators: *Magic Moments: This Worked for Me.* She was a winner in the following contests: *Lillian Dean, NightWriters Annual Fiction,* and *Writer's Digest* in fiction, non-fiction, and poetry categories. Website: www.annaunkovich.com.

Kalila Volkov is the author of *Fishing for Equilibrium, The Power of a Diary,* as well as the holiday stories: *Kentucky Fried Christmas, Holiday Tenderness,* and *Christmas Kaleidoscope,* which appeared in the *Tolosa Press* publications. Several of her poems have been published as well. She enjoys performing with Canzona Women's Ensemble and Cuesta Master Chorale. Kalila is excited to bring her children's book, *Hiking Trail Treasure Land,* to print soon.

Rebecca Waddell works for the beautiful county of San Luis Obispo, but writing and her two daughters are her true passions. When she isn't working on her middle grade and young adult novels, she enjoys dabbling in short stories and poetry. Her motto is: *If I don't write, untold numbers of fictional characters will die!*

T. C. West writes when inspiration, time to reflect on experience, and hours free from pressing tasks or obligations combine to allow production. Poems and prose in the form of memoir, speculative fiction, newspaper columns, parables, and audio scripts have all emerged when a tendency to procrastinate is suppressed by an attractive deadline. The seismic chart of T.C.'s life shows a few periods of relative calm interrupted by unpredictable cataclysmic events. So far she survived.

Dennis Eamon Young, a native of Brooklyn, New York, is a professional photographer, artist, and writer. He moved to San Luis Obispo in 2007 to marry and pursue artistic interests, meet interesting people, and take on new and exciting challenges. He practices tai chi loves, travelling, photographing events, telling and writing stories, reading, and learning. Dennis enjoys working with good people from non-profit to corporate, as he attempts to make life better and enjoy its bounty.

Liu Yu is a former member of the Jiangsu Province Professional Wushu Team and a graduate of Beijing University of Physical Education. Her memoir, *Awakening the Sleeping Tiger: The True Story of a Professional Chinese Athlete*, reveals the rigors of Chinese sports training and a hidden side of the Chinese culture. She is a former U.S. Wushu Team Coach and the current owner of the Wushu Taichi Center in San Luis Obispo, CA.

Made in the USA
San Bernardino, CA
30 June 2014